Information Assurance and Risk Management Strategies

Manage Your Information Systems and Tools in the Cloud

Bradley Fowler

Information Assurance and Risk Management Strategies: Manage Your Information Systems and Tools in the Cloud

Bradley Fowler
Canton, MI, USA

ISBN-13 (pbk): 978-1-4842-9741-4
https://doi.org/10.1007/978-1-4842-9742-1

ISBN-13 (electronic): 978-1-4842-9742-1

Managing Director, Apress Media LLC: Welmoed Spahr
Acquisitions Editor: Celestin Suresh John
Development Editor: James Markham
Coordinating Editor: Mark Powers
Copy Editor: Mary Behr

Cover designed by eStudioCalamar
Cover image designed by Freepik (www.freepik.com)

Distributed to the book trade worldwide by Apress Media, LLC, 1 New York Plaza, New York, NY 10004, U.S.A. Phone 1-800-SPRINGER, fax (201) 348-4505, e-mail orders-ny@springer-sbm.com, or visit www.springeronline.com. Apress Media, LLC is a California LLC and the sole member (owner) is Springer Science + Business Media Finance Inc (SSBM Finance Inc). SSBM Finance Inc is a **Delaware** corporation.

For information on translations, please e-mail booktranslations@springernature.com; for reprint, paperback, or audio rights, please e-mail bookpermissions@springernature.com.

Apress titles may be purchased in bulk for academic, corporate, or promotional use. eBook versions and licenses are also available for most titles. For more information, reference our Print and eBook Bulk Sales web page at www.apress.com/bulk-sales.

Any source code or other supplementary material referenced by the author in this book is available to readers on GitHub (https://github.com/Apress). For more detailed information, please visit https://www.apress.com/gp/services/source-code.

Paper in this product is recyclable

Dedicated to Clarence E. "Butch" "Road-Runner" Fowler.
As I live so do you.

Table of Contents

About the Author

Bradley Fowler earned a Graduate Certificate in Information Assurance at the University of Maryland Global Campus and a Master of Science in Cloud Computing Architecture from the University of Maryland Global Campus, magnum cum laude. Prior to earning these credentials, he earned a Master of Science in Cybersecurity and Master of Science in Managing Information Systems in Information Security Management, both from Bellevue University, summa cum laude. He is currently finishing his Doctor of Education Administration at California Coast University, Doctor of Management in Information Systems and Technology at the University of Phoenix, and PhD in Cybersecurity Leadership at Capitol Technology University. He is lifetime member of the Golden Key International Honor Society, the National Cybersecurity Alliance, the National Cybersecurity Student Association, a peer review panelist for the *Cybersecurity Skills Journal*, and a member of the Global Tech Council. He is a general member of the Alumni Council for the American Public University System. He is also a joint author of *Cybersecurity Public Policy SWOT Analysis for 43 Countries* and the writer of *AWS for Public and Private Sectors: Cloud Computing Architecture for Government and Business* (Apress, 2023).

Bradley's favorite activities are weightlifting, roller skating, going on trips, cooking, creating non-fiction and fiction stories, and riding roller coasters.

Contact Bradley Fowler at `doctorbrad@email.phoenix.edu` for invitations to speak at conferences, public or private sector speaking engagements, lectures, webinars, and consulting.

About the Technical Reviewer

Mr. Amir Mukeri is currently working as Senior Engineering Manager, Data Science for Qualys Security. He holds B.E. (Information Technology) and M.E. (Computer Engineering) degrees from SP Pune University, India. He has more than 16 years of experience working with technology companies in India and the US in the domains of cloud, storage and disaster recovery, security, and AI/ML.
He has multiple research publications in peer reviewed international journals to his credit in the areas of AI/ML, cybersecurity, and adversarial machine learning. He has a patent for a cloud-based disaster recovery region recommendation system.

Introduction

This book focuses on Berkshire Hathaway Inc., a Fortune 500 corporation, as an example of how to effectively initiate, execute, manage, monitor, and update information assurance and risk management strategies to secure corporate information systems, technology, and the cloud. Using publicly known and reported data from the Security and Exchange Commission, including the 2022 Berkshire Hathaway Inc. Annual Report, this framework of information assurance risk management strategies is an example that can be applied to any corporate information system, technology, or cloud computing architecture. This tool of knowledge is designed to help support you, an ISTC (information systems, technology, and cloud) practitioner, and your need to implement effective information assurance and risk management strategies. This resource enables you to understand how to define an effective information assurance and risk management strategy that offers the ability to protect the information assets of your corporate environment. This research shares key components to effectively assess and conduct information system security analysis, including developing clearly written and researched Information Usage Profiles that provide a clear outline of a corporation's valued information (i.e., customer records, trademarks, patents, employee records, vendor third-party records, software assets, hardware assets, information system assets, cloud assets, and physical security assets). This profile also provides a detailed description of these corporate assets and level of sensitivity, and it outlines how information assets are utilized. It also details the information asset usage and storing methods.

This research enables you as an ISTC practitioner to comprehend the laws and policies enacted, domestically and internationally, regarding information security assets. Gaining this knowledge can improve how you outline internal policies for information assurance, information systems, information technology, and cloud environments.

CHAPTER 1

Information Assurance Analysis

Classroom demonstration of analysis

Learning objectives:

- Understand what information assurance is.

- Understand why information assurance is critical for business.

- Understand how to improve information assurance risk management strategies.

1

© Bradley Fowler 2023
B. Fowler, *Information Assurance and Risk Management Strategies*,
https://doi.org/10.1007/978-1-4842-9742-1_1

- Understand the importance of creating and managing an information usage profile.

- Understand risk factors.

In this chapter, you will gain essential knowledge to help improve the way you view and adopt information assurance in the workplace. Understanding information assurance is important. But knowing how to effectively assess, implement, and manage information assurance is key to winning the war against cybercriminals. In fact, when attempting to out think cybercriminals, it is essential to understand who your enemy is and what strategies you need to implement to deter and thwart their malicious attack methods. Knowing this is half your battle. Thus, in this chapter, you will learn why information assurance is important to business. You will be introduced to a method of improving information assurance using risk management strategies. You will also learn how to create an information usage profile. Most importantly, you will be introduced to a risk factor table to help you better outline your own risk factor table for your enterprise, business, or organization.

Information Assurance Primer

Information assurance is vital to managing the confidentiality, integrity, and availability of information assets. No matter what method of storage is used for information assets, implementing quality information assurance is vital to ethical management of information. This includes the procedures deployed to maintain the confidentiality of the information. Confidentiality of information supports privacy of sensitive details that identify individuals, such as their name, address, birth date, social security number, credit card numbers, bank information, and medical health information. Integrity in information assurance provides a framework of truth and validity that enables the information to be utilized for professional and personal purposes, without being invalid and biased. When information is without integrity, there is a risk that the information is misleading and biased. Bias in information establishes dishonesty. When information assurance embodies confidentiality, integrity, and availability, it aligns with the recommendations for information security practices and procedures deployed by the National Security Agency and the U.S. Department of Homeland Security.

Are you aware of how easy it is today to gain access to corporate information regarding information systems, technology, and the cloud? Anyone anywhere on the planet with a computer, WIFI, Internet, and a willingness to research can gain access to enough information to acquire knowledge of known security vulnerabilities associated with any software and hardware application a corporation relies upon. To explain this better, I used D & B Hoovers, which anyone can access, to gain information regarding a corporation's description. It delivers details about the type of business being conducted, the partnerships established, and a business ranking. D & B Hoovers provides details regarding what industry the company is listed under and a headquarters address, including hyperlinks to any listed corporate website. This information helps social engineers and cybercriminals understand how many employees are essential to the business' primary operations; plus essential information is provided about the corporation's geographical locations. Additional information includes details about revenue earnings, financial statements, and annual revenue of the prior year, income before taxes, net income, and diluted EPS. When a social engineer is building a profile for a target corporation, they can utilize the Security Exchange Commission website, which provides a corporation's annual report pursuant to Section 13 or 15 (d) of the Security Exchange Act of 1934. This report includes an 8-K current report, Form 10-K annual report, and 10-Q quarterly report as well as proxy annual meeting details, information statements, and ownership disclosures. With the 10-K annual report, cybercriminals can learn about the risk factors the corporation shares with the public. For example, Berkshire Hathaway Inc. shares details about its general business risks, including concerns about terrorist acts that could hurt its operating businesses and cybersecurity risk factors. Berkshire Hathaway also reports that cybercriminals who deploy attacks against its systems could cause a loss of assets and critical information, plus expose the corporation to remediation costs and reputational damage. [1] Furthermore, this report delivers knowledge regarding previous cyberattack incidents that were obviously successful. Berkshire Hathaway admits that any type of technology attack can significantly disrupt business operations or cause failure of its technology, including service interruptions, safety failures, security issues, and regulatory compliance failures to create an inability to effectively protect information assets from unauthorized users as well as create additional operational challenges. [2]

Even scarier is knowing that cybercriminals can learn about the technology software and hardware devices Berkshire Hathaway relies on for each business office, by researching these facts. For instance, Berkshire Hathaway offers consumers many energy sources, including wind, natural gas, coal, solar, hydroelectric, nuclear, and geothermal. Each energy source has its own number of consumers who purchase such services from Berkshire Hathaway. This enables cyber criminals to increase target profile data to learn more about each extended business service Berkshire Hathaway delivers and thus gain knowledge of the technology tools relied on by each of these service offices. Berkshire Hathaway also offers retail, manufacturing services, real estate, training facilities, production facilities, and distribution centers. Each of these extended branches relies on information systems and technology within the Berkshire Hathaway business architect and ecosystem. These explicitly shared details can become instrumental in supporting cybercriminals in deploying a cyberattack against Berkshire Hathaway and its extended subsidiaries. To help control the risk of publicly shared information assets, Berkshire Hathaway must implement effective information assurance risk management strategies tailored for its corporate information systems and technology reliance.

Thus, the first step in learning how to improve the information assurance risk management strategies for corporate information systems and technology is to analyze the business usage and reliance on information and information systems and information technology. This includes understanding the factor analysis of information risk, asset identification, hardware assets, subsystems and software assets, cloud-based information assets, virtual assets, information assets, asset classification, and data classification. Clearly, information systems, technology, and cloud (ISTC) practitioners working in corporate offices need to define Information Usage Profile tables (IUP). The IUP table should share categories of information such as customers records, vendor records, employee records, trademarks, patents, software assets, hardware assets, information systems assets, cloud assets, and physical security assets. This IUP should also include a description of the information assets, level of sensitivity of the information, how the information asset is used or processed, and all ISTC information systems, technology, and cloud usage or storing capabilities. Table 1-1 provides a clearly designed IUP.

Table 1-1. *Information Usage Profile*

Category of information	Description of the information asset(s)	Sensitivity of the information	How is this information used or processed?	IT assets using or storing this information
Customer records	Name, address, birthdate, driver's license, bank routing information	Strict confidentiality	To process orders, fulfill service obligations, maintain records, process payments	Computers (desktops/laptops), servers, cloud VPCs, physical filing systems, external hard drive storage, and software
Trademarks	Brand logos and designs	Confidentiality	Legal ownership, liability suits	External hard drives, cloud VPNs, computers (desktops/laptops)
Patents	Models and methods of product development/ service development	Confidentiality	Registered with federal court systems and state legal systems to identify brand products or services	External hard drives, software, computers (desktops/laptops), servers, cloud VPCs
Employee records	Name, salary, birthdate, bank direct deposit details, investment information, stock details, 401K, health and medical insurance	Confidentiality	Manage employee's records for salary, company investments, and liability insurance	External hard drives, CRM software, computers (desktops/laptops), servers, and cloud VPCs

(continued)

Table 1-1. (*continued*)

Category of information	Description of the information asset(s)	Sensitivity of the information	How is this information used or processed?	IT assets using or storing this information
Vendor and third-party records	Name, contact person, address, phone number, payment details, and banking information	Confidentiality	Utilized to maintain records of consumers' credit card information and banking information	External hard drive, software, USB drives, computers (desktops/laptops), servers, and cloud VPCs
Software assets	Customer names, order numbers, tracking numbers, item numbers, credit card information, passwords, and shipping address details	Strict confidentiality	Develop, transmit, and store data files, order numbers, tracking information, backup, and archiving details	Internal software, USB drives, desktops/laptops
Hardware assets	System backup and archive, storage files, and RAM	Strict confidentiality	Transmit data files internally and externally	Desktops/laptops, servers, networks, WIFI, and Internet
Information systems assets	Product files, customer files, business transactions, payroll, and CRM	Strict confidentiality	Store, transmit, and secure data files internally and externally	Telecommunications, WIFI, Internet, servers, and networks
Cloud assets	VPNs, servers, IAM, and machine learning	Strict confidentiality	Store and transmit data files securely	Server, network, and key pairs

(*continued*)

Table 1-1. (*continued*)

Category of information	Description of the information asset(s)	Sensitivity of the information	How is this information used or processed?	IT assets using or storing this information
Physical security assets	Entrance access cards, biometrics, printers, fax machines, supplies, desktop monitors, desktop computers, and laptops	Strict confidentiality	Protects employees, Human Resource offices and cubes, company supplies, and internal sensitive data resources	Entrance doors into the physical office

The next important step is creating a risk analysis. For Berkshire Hathaway, I defined the risk analysis using three analysis formats. The first analysis format describes Berkshire Hathaway's needs or requirements for IT security. This analysis conveys the likely sources of threats or attacks for each type of information or business operation and explains the type of information and/or business operations that need to be protected, including identifying and discussing the sources of information utilized in this analysis. The second analysis presents a risk profile in table format. I include an introduction paragraph to convey the risk profile, including information contained in the table and the sources utilized to obtain this information. The third analysis provides a summary of the risk analysis, the identified risk, and potential impact of risks Berkshire Hathaway faces.

Analysis One

Berkshire Hathaway relies on information security as a method to protect sensitive information assets internally and externally. Berkshire Hathaway's total corporate family membership includes 6521 company names. [3] Each corporate family membership's physical location hosts sensitive data on the information system, including virtual servers. Information hosted on these information systems includes names, client lists, addresses, phone numbers, email addresses, email responses, internet search history, documents containing names and account numbers, information regarding trademark

7

secrets, intellectual property, and financial resources as well as deeds of properties. In-office WIFI supports the usage of the Internet to transmit documents across public or private cloud infrastructure hosted by a third-party service provider. Each employee connected to one of the 6521 company names listed on the D & B Hoover website utilizes the Berkshire Hathaway computer network, including the LAN (local area network), WAN (wide-area network), and WLAN (wireless local area network). The LAN, WAN, and WLAN are gateways for system intrusion. For instance, data transmitted across a WLAN enables an intruder to attack the wireless client in a peer-to-peer fashion. This attack method enables the intruder access to the corporation computer network simply using a legitimate client as an accepted entry point. [4] Vulnerabilities embedded in the WAN can also be an entrance gateway for hackers to steer traffic and shut down networks. Wireless network attacks include **parking lot attacks**, **drive-by attacks**, **wardriving**, **warchalking**, **bluesnarfing**, **bluejacking**, **bluebugging**, and **evil twin attacks**.

The fax machine is connected to the WIFI to support transmission and receiving of documents. This too creates another access point for a cyberattack. In fact, fax numbers are easy to acquire. Once acquired, attackers can send malicious content in image files by fax to a potential victim. [5]

The printer is also connected to a computer that is connected to the WIFI. Like any network device, if printers are not properly managed and configured, they can expose sensitive data to anyone who gains unauthorized access to exploit sensitive information. [6] Moreover, the WIFI can create another vulnerability. Research explains how these tools are a security risk. In fact, Howard Solomon reported that small business administrators utilizing Cisco routers were at risk for **website redirects**. [7] Solomon also reported that many vulnerabilities can enable remote attackers to deploy denial-of-service (DoS) attacks or gain access to devices and execute horrible malicious activities. It is publicly known that Berkshire Hathaway relies on Cisco routers; this information is reported in the D & B Hoover Technologies in Use list.

With 6521 corporate names operating businesses on behalf of Berkshire Hathaway, it is imperative that security configurations be audited on every technology tool used. Vulnerabilities can be points of entrance for intrusion and/or a cyberattack, ransomware, malware, or virus that can cause irreversible damage. Also, the access key cards provided to employees to gain access to the facilities, offices, and enterprises located in various geographical regions of the United States can be external pathways to internal information systems. In fact, each of the 6521 offices Berkshire Hathaway owns or operates business endeavors from utilizes Microsoft Windows OSes (i.e., 7, 8, 10, or 11). The Cybersecurity & Infrastructure Security Agency explains that Microsoft

Windows has incorrectly parsed shortcuts that enable malicious code to be executed when the operating system displays the icon of a malicious shortcut file. This enables an attacker to successfully exploit the vulnerabilities and execute code as the logged-on user. [8] Furthermore, it is publicly known that Berkshire Hathaway relies on Microsoft Windows Server and Server 2008, which are outdated and vulnerable for attack. Research revealed that Microsoft Windows Common Log File System driver embodies an unspecified vulnerability that can enable privilege escalation. [9] Because Berkshire Hathaway and its 6521 companies utilize Google Chrome and Microsoft Edge browsers, which the Cybersecurity Infrastructure Security Agency reports embodies insufficient data validation vulnerabilities, this impacts another layer of assumed security.

Analysis Two

This risk analysis is a risk profile that conveys the likely sources of threats and attacks associated with each type of information or business operation Berkshire Hathaway, depends on for business operations. Table 1-1 shows risks factors and provides a description of the risk and risk categories as well as the impact of such risk. Thus, to increase security, Berkshire Hathaway must assess all vulnerabilities mentioned and implement patching and mitigation methods. This will decrease some of the known risks and provide additional layers of security. To help explain this research, D & B Hoover created a SWOT Analysis on Berkshire Hathaway, reporting the information technology assets and security threats that could impact the corporation's reputation and its financial stability. After all, Berkshire Hathaway relies on information systems, technology, and the cloud for information sharing transactions, including credit card payments and telecommunication. Such technology can expose Berkshire Hathaway and its 6521 entities to online theft and cybercrime, including hacking. And when Berkshire Hathaway implements security methods to deter or decrease successful cyberattacks or cyberincidents, vulnerabilities still exist, both known and unknown. The extent of internet security is dependent on the quality of the hardware and software used, which may not protect the company's portal from unauthorized attacks, resulting in break-ins and other disruptive system failures. [10] Thus, ISTC practitioners should increase usage of a risk factor table to understand what is at risk and to categorize the risks and the impact levels of such risks. Table 1-2 represents Berkshire Hathaway's risk factors.

Table 1-2. *Risk Factors*

Risk ID	Risk Title	Description	Risk Category	Impact Level
001	Information extortion	Ransomware deployed to retrieve information assets via known vulnerable technology tools. Berkshire Hathaway reports that terrorist acts can hinder its business operations.	EXTREMELY HIGH	Catastrophic
002	Human error or failure	Employees accidentally open an embedded link in an email sent from a known person, who is not the actual sender. This is considered spoofing. Berkshire Hathaway reports that it needs qualified personnel to operate its businesses.	HIGH	Major
003	Compromise of intellectual property	External attackers gain access to the network via a known vulnerability and retrieve data files from an unsecure computer device.	Medium	Moderate
004	Technical hardware failures or installation errors	The hardware lacks required updates and enables attackers to gain access to computers, networks, information systems, the cloud, or IT. Berkshire Hathaway classifies this as a cybersecurity attack risk.	HIGH	Catastrophic

(continued)

Table 1-2. (*continued*)

Risk ID	Risk Title	Description	Risk Category	Impact Level
005	Technical software failures or installation errors	Installed software applications are infused with known vulnerabilities that can impede security vulnerabilities woven in the current information system, network, hardware, cloud infrastructure, and mobile or WIFI. Berkshire Hathaway considers these risks as cybersecurity issues.	HIGH	Major
006	Technological obsolescence	Products or services are no longer required and are replaced with new versions.	HIGH	Major
007	Sabotage or vandalism	Former employees wreak havoc on the external and internal landscape of the enterprise and destroy USB drives, cut cords, and write negative reports online.	Medium	Moderate
008	Forces of nature	Tornadoes, power outages, hurricanes, floods, and windstorms. Berkshire Hathaway lists these events as climate change issues.	Medium	Major
009	Theft	Employees steal computers, USB drives, monitors, mobile devices, files, customer data, account numbers, etc.	Medium	Major
010	Software attacks	Application programming interfaces are installed with known vulnerabilities that can be used to exploit the business and share private information.	HIGH	Major

(*continued*)

Table 1-2. (*continued*)

Risk ID	Risk Title	Description	Risk Category	Impact Level
011	Vendor and third-party records	Files of vendor names, addresses, and account numbers can be stolen and sold for monetary gain.	HIGH	LOW
012	Information system assets	Retrieval of employee's names, addresses, salary, and bank routing numbers can be used for malicious purposes.	HIGH	Major
013	Cloud assets	Retrieval of sensitive enterprise data such as stocks, banking accounts, and financial transactions as well as enterprise information system assets including passwords and multifactor authentication data.	HIGH	Medium
014	Telecommunications	Communication channels targeted for covert surveillance include everything from phone lines and online chat to mobile phone data.	HIGH	Major
015	Physical	Entrance access cards, biometrics, printers, fax machines, supplies, and desktop monitors, desktop computers, and laptops each can be hacked, stolen, or manipulated to enable cyberattacks or other forms of sabotage. Berkshire Hathaway lists this with property and casualty insurance loss.	HIGH	Major

Berkshire Hathaway's risk factors differ from other corporations but using this table as a model enables ISTC practitioners to increase risk management and begin controlling risk factors that create vulnerabilities within corporate information systems, technologies, and the cloud.

Analysis Three

Berkshire Hathaway has a tremendous burden of protecting and securing its information assets from cyberattacks, cyberterrorists, cyberhacktivists, cyberespionage, and cybercriminals. Berkshire Hathaway's listed technologies on the D & B Hoover website provides cybercriminals enough information to compile a profile to support their ability to exploit any known vulnerability integrated in each of the software applications. To deter successful exploitation of these known vulnerabilities, Berkshire Hathaway's IT practitioners need to stay current in understanding how to patch and mitigate each individual technology tool, software, and hardware relied upon. This includes effectively writing and managing clear reports with the name of the reporter conducting the audit, date, and time stamp, plus an outline of all issues, vulnerabilities, steps, and procedures deployed, and a brief explanation of why steps and procedures were implemented. This written record explains to the executive leaders, managers, and stakeholders the details of what is being done to stay current in protecting and managing the information system, technology, and cloud environment for the enterprise. It is also important that Berkshire Hathaway increase quarterly assessments of its IT practitioners, making sure each one responsible for overseeing and managing their information system, technology, and cloud environments stays current in credential earnings. This keeps the team knowledgeable and capable of performing all tasks efficiently. For instance, in the 10-K SEC report for 2021, Berkshire Hathaway reported that cybersecurity risks could result in service interruptions, office security failures, office security events, legal and policy compliance failures, and an inability to effectively protect its information assets against unauthorized users as well as additional operational difficulties. Cybercriminals could deploy attacks against the information systems, which could result in a loss of assets and critical information as well as expose Berkshire Hathaway to remediation costs and reputational damage. [11]

Thus, it is recommended Berkshire Hathaway implement effective assessments and auditing of all technology tools utilized, quarterly or as needed, to increase security and decrease the potential risks embedded within the information system, technology, and cloud environment. This will require Berkshire Hathaway to hire effectively trained and qualified technologists who understand the needs of the enterprise and its reliance on technology. Otherwise, the enterprise and its subsidiaries will remain vulnerable and continue being easily victimized by cybercriminals.

Case Study

Berkshire Hathaway recently hired a senior level IT practitioner who had been working for a competitor. The new IT practitioner has experience with network administration responsibilities and has implemented a strategy to assess the level of threat that currently is embodied in the network, including the computers and software. However, the IT practitioner doesn't implement system updates on the computers for each employee. Nor does the IT practitioner maintain updates on any of the software utilized, as recommended by the software developer.

There is a consistent deployment of cyberattacks targeting a branch of Berkshire Hathaway's business operations that works with a list of 160,000 clients. The software used to manage the information assets of these clients is a third-party software application. The IT practitioner does not maintain a close partnership of communication with the third-party software service and product provider, which increases the chance for this software to be a gateway entrance for cyberattackers to gain access to this information.

No one in the office has knowledge that vulnerabilities are woven into the third-party software. And the IT practitioner does not stay current with the recommended patching strategies shared in the Common Vulnerabilities and Exposure website. Unfortunately, a successful cyberattack occurs and the third-party software that is relied on to manage the information assets of the 160,000 clients is the entrance point that supported this cyberattack. How should the IT practitioner respond once the attack is discovered? Who should the IT practitioner report this incident to?

In any given situation, the IT practitioner is solely responsible for managing the organization's information system, technology, and cloud. If the IT practitioner is not doing what they are required to do, who is to blame for this attack? No other office worker has the knowledge or skills to safeguard the information systems, technology, and cloud. What can Berkshire Hathaway do to deter and thwart the next attack?

Summary

In this chapter, you gained essential details to help you understand what information assurance is and why information assurance is an important asset for business development and communication. You also learned the impact information assurance has in alignment with reliance on technology tools, including software, hardware, and cloud environments. Most importantly, you learned the value of developing an

Information Usage Profile (IUP). This profile is invaluable because it provides details about key business information including customers records, vendor records, employee records, trademarks, patents, software assets, hardware assets, information systems assets, cloud assets, and physical security assets. The IUP should include a description of the information assets, level of sensitivity of the information, and explain how the information asset is utilized and/or processed. It should list all ISTC information systems, technology, and cloud usage or storing capabilities. You also learned about risk analysis and the role this plays in a corporation's ability to implement effective information assurance. Developing a good risk analysis enables the corporation to describe the needs and requirements for IT and information assurance security. This analysis provides knowledge of the likeliness of the source of threats or cyberattacks that could impact business operations. Finally, you learned that a risk analysis enables you to identify risk and potential impact of risks a corporation faces.

Discussion Questions

1. What is information assurance?

2. Why is information assurance important to business information security?

3. What is social engineering?

4. Why is an information usage profile important?

5. What is a parking lot attack?

6. What is a drive-by attack?

7. What is wardriving?

8. What is warchalking?

9. What is bluesnarfing?

10. What is bluejacking?

11. What is bluebugging?

12. What is an evil twin attack?

13. Why should you create and maintain a risk factor table?

Keywords

Social engineering, parking lot attack, drive-by attack, wardriving, warchalking, bluesnarfing, bluejacking, bluebugging, evil twin attack, website redirects, and denial-of-service attacks

CHAPTER 2

Information Risk Management and Analysis Strategies

Risk factor scale

© Bradley Fowler 2023
B. Fowler, *Information Assurance and Risk Management Strategies*,
https://doi.org/10.1007/978-1-4842-9742-1_2

Learning objectives:

- Understand how to assess known information risk within your organization.

- Understand why using an information risk mitigation security strategy control profile is important.

- Understand the information sensitivity risk within your organization.

- Understand how to effectively mitigate information risk management for your organization.

Previously, I covered the technology tools, software, hardware, and network infrastructure that Berkshire Hathaway relies on for business communications and operations. You also learned how Berkshire Hathaway presents itself to consumers and the public, and you gained information about Berkshire Hathaway investor relations, including a comparison on how the corporation represents itself to investors and shareholders in comparison with how it presents itself on its customer web interface. Additionally, you learned about the Berkshire Hathaway 10-K Annual Report and acquired details about the corporation's information assets, subsystems, software assets, and hardware assets as well as how these assets are utilized to conduct business operations. Furthermore, I provided a detailed information profile chart of Berkshire Hathaway to identify categories of information that need to be protected against losses of confidentiality, integrity, and availability. This profile contained distinct categories of information, including a description of the information assets, level of sensitivity of the information, how this information is used or processed, the IT assets and how they are used, and details regarding methods of storing this information. I also shared details regarding the hardware assets, software assets, information system security assets, network component assets, and people assets. I also provided details conveying the type of information Berkshire Hathaway collects, processes, transmits, and stores as a part of its business operations. Most importantly, I shared details conveying the type of information technology and systems Berkshire Hathaway utilizes to accomplish business objectives plus details about the type of information required to operate these systems.

Now I'm sharing information regarding the risk management strategies that your organization should consider after reviewing this risk management strategy designed for Berkshire Hathaway to reduce known risks and vulnerabilities in the technology relied on and utilized. Following the recommendations rendered in NIST 800-53 and the NIST Cybersecurity Framework, I provide information about the functions, categories, and subcategories that should be considered when mitigating risks, which was discussed in Chapter 1. In this chapter, you will review four distinct tables that convey a list of risks concerns commonly integrated with technology tools, software, and hardware relied on for business operations and business communication. Reviewing the contents of each table will provide guidance for you to mirror to begin modifying your current approach to technology risk management and analysis strategies that can improve the security of each risk factor known within your organization. The first table includes risk associated with **information extortion**, human error, compromise of intellectual property, technical hardware failures or installation errors, technical software failures or installation errors, **technological obsolescence**, sabotage or vandalism, forces of nature, theft, software attacks, vendor and third-party records, information system assets, cloud assets, telecommunications, and the physical infrastructure of the business environment. The second table details the information sensitivity risk and outlines what risk concerns should be addressed and how to effectively address such risk. Aligning your organization's information sensitivity risk profile with this outline will decrease known risks associated with these risk factors and increase training awareness focus points for you to improve the overall security of these risk factors in your organization. The third table guides you towards defining a clearly written information sensitivity risk profile. The fourth table highlights risk factors from high to low to help you comprehend how severe a risk is and how to control risk factors that align with the known vulnerability risk factors engulfed in the primary risk mitigation security control profile. Looking at Table 2-1, you can begin to understand what risk factors you should list in your own risk factor table. Describing these key factors will provide enough details for executive members and stakeholders to gain a better understanding of the risks associated with business operations and communication. The risk category ranking helps you to determine what level of risk each risk factor has as well as the impact of each risk factor level.

Table 2-1. *Risk Factors*

Risk ID	Risk title	Description	Risk category	Impact level
001	Information extortion	Ransomware is deployed to retrieve information assets via known vulnerable technology tools. Berkshire Hathaway reports that terrorist acts can hinder its business operations. [1]	EXTREMELY HIGH	Catastrophic
002	Human error or failure	Employees accidentally open an embedded link in an email sent from a known person, who is not the actual sender. This is considered spoofing. Berkshire Hathaway reports that it needs qualified personnel to operate its businesses. [2]	HIGH	Major
003	Compromise of intellectual property	External attackers gain access to the network via a known vulnerability and retrieve data files from an unsecure computer device.	Medium	Moderate
004	Technical hardware failures or installation errors	Hardware lacks required updates and enables attackers to gain access to the computer, network, information systems, the cloud, or IT. Berkshire Hathaway classifies this as a cybersecurity attack risk. [3]	HIGH	Catastrophic
005	Technical software failures or installation errors	Software applications are infused with known vulnerabilities that can impede security vulnerabilities woven in the current information system, network, hardware, cloud infrastructure, and mobile or WIFI. Berkshire Hathaway considers these risks as cybersecurity issues.	HIGH	Major
006	Technological obsolescence	Products or services are no longer required and are replaced with new versions.	HIGH	Major

(continued)

Table 2-1. (*continued*)

Risk ID	Risk title	Description	Risk category	Impact level
007	Sabotage or vandalism	Former employees wreak havoc on the external and internal landscape of the enterprise and destroy USB drives, cut cords, and write negative reports online.	Medium	Moderate
008	Forces of nature	Tornadoes, power outages, hurricane, floods, and windstorms. Berkshire Hathaway lists these events as climate change issues. [4]	Medium	Major
009	Theft	Employees steal computers, USB drives, monitors, mobile devices, files, customer data, account numbers, etc.	Medium	Major
010	Software attacks	Application programming interfaces are installed with known vulnerabilities that exploit the business and share private information.	HIGH	Major
011	Vendor and third-party records	Files of vendor names, addresses, and account numbers can be stolen and sold for monetary gain.	HIGH	LOW
012	Information system assets	Retrieval of employee's names, addresses, salary, and bank routing numbers can be used for malicious purposes.	HIGH	Major
013	Cloud assets	Retrieval of sensitive enterprise data such as stocks, banking accounts, and financial transactions as well as enterprise information system assets, including passwords and multifactor authentication data.	HIGH	Medium

(*continued*)

Table 2-1. (*continued*)

Risk ID	Risk title	Description	Risk category	Impact level
014	Tele-communications	Communication channels targeted for covert surveillance include everything from phone lines and online chat to mobile phone data.	HIGH	Major
015	Physical	Entrance access cards, biometrics, printers, fax machines, supplies, desktop monitors, desktop computers, and laptops each can be hacked, stolen, or manipulated to enable cyberattacks or other forms of sabotage. Berkshire Hathaway lists this with property and casualty insurance loss. [5]	HIGH	Major

This table enables you to understand that Berkshire Hathaway relies on business procedures and processes that need effective management strategies and clearly written policies to support the organization's mission, goals, and objectives. When effective security controls are implemented, such as firewalls, intrusion detection systems, and policies, the level of vulnerabilities can be reduced and the inability to exploit these known vulnerabilities decreases, which lowers the cost for security and increases the ability to protect the organization's reputation from damage. This also helps decrease civil and criminal liabilities that can impact the economic stability of the organization.

In Table 2-2, you will review a list of risk factors I assessed with concern regarding how to improve risk management and better control the potential security risk associated with daily business operations, including usage and reliance of information systems, technology, and the cloud. Keep in mind that all risk management strategies provided align with the security controls enacted by the National Institute of Standards and Technology, which are enveloped in their 800 special series publications.

Table 2-2. *Risk Mitigation Strategies Security Controls Profile*

Risk ID	Risk title	Risk mitigation strategy	CSF category ID	Security controls
001	Information extortion	Implementing role-based access controls will reduce the risk of unauthorized access to customer information by controlling which individuals are granted access to the systems and software used to collect, process, transmit, and store this information.	PR.AC Identity Management, Authentication, and Access Control: PR.AC-4	AC-3 (7) Access Enforcement I Role Based Access Control; AC-3 (11) Access Enforcement I Restrict Access to Specific Information Types
002	Human error or failure	Integrate improved awareness training for personnel to gain knowledge of the risk associated with human error.	PR. AT Awareness & Training RS.CO Communications	SP 800-30 SP 800-39 Information Security COBIT 5
003	Compromise of intellectual property	Implement effective security controls that protect data at rest and limits who has access.	ID.AM Asset Management ID. RA Risk Assessment PR. IP Information Protection Processes and Procedures	FISMA Integrity CNSSI 4009 Insider Threat Programming SP 800-63-3 SP 800-30

(continued)

Table 2-2. (*continued*)

Risk ID	Risk title	Risk mitigation strategy	CSF category ID	Security controls
004	Technical hardware failures or installation errors	Managing hardware updates as recommended by the manufacturer will decrease failures and installation errors.	ID. RA Risk Assessment PR.MA Maintenance, RC.RP Recovery Planning	CNSSI-4009 FIPS 199 SP 800-128
005	Technical software failures or installation errors	Assuring manufacturing recommendations are aligned with the deployment of software updates to reduce software failures.	RC.IM Improvement DE.AE Anomalies and Events DE. DP Detection Processes RS.AN Analysis RS.MI Mitigation	FISMA SP 800-128 OMB A-130 CNSSI 4009
006	Technological obsolescence	Manage effective system updates that remain current with technology upgrades, modifications, and omissions.	RC. IM Improvement RS.AN Analysis DE. DP Detection Processes PR.MA Maintenance ID.RA Risk Assessment	SP 800-128 SP 800-37 OMB A-130 USC 3502
007	Sabotage or vandalism	Assess all software and hardware effectively, and conduct audits to ensure no access is granted to unauthorized personnel.	DE.AE Anomalies and Events DE.CM Security Continuous Monitoring DE. DP Detection Processes	SP 800-37 CNSSI 4009 OMB-A130 SP 800-30

(*continued*)

Table 2-2. (*continued*)

Risk ID	Risk title	Risk mitigation strategy	CSF category ID	Security controls
008	Forces of nature	Increasing personnel awareness training that prepares them to flee as needed and continue working as required, remotely.	PR.AT Awareness Training DA.AE. Anomalies and Events RS.RP Response Planning RS.CO Communication RC.RP Recovery Planning	CNSSI 4009 SP 800-154 SP 800-39 FIPS 199
009	Theft	Increase internal physical security and make sure an access-as-needed policy is implemented to protect sensitive information assets.	PR.AC Identity Management and Access Control PR.DS Data Security DE. DP Detection Processes	FIPS 201-2 OMB A-130 FIPS 200 CNSSI 4009 SP 800-39
010	Software attacks	Maintain aggressive system updates to decrease unauthorized access to software.	ID.RA Risk Assessment PR.MA Maintenance PR. PT Protective Technology DE.CM Security Continuous Monitoring	SP 800-39 CNSSI 4009 SP 800-128 SP 800-30 SP 800-154

(*continued*)

Table 2-2. *(continued)*

Risk ID	Risk title	Risk mitigation strategy	CSF category ID	Security controls
011	Vendor and third-party records	Ensure that vendor and third-party records align with the enterprise security policy and federal recommended guidelines under NIST SP 800 series publications.	ID.BE Business Environments ID.SC Supply Chain Risk Management DE. DP Detection Processes	USC 552 ISO 15288 SP 800-39 CNSSI 4009
012	Information system assets	Implement an information system policy that controls access and authorization using multifactor authentication and encryption on data at rest and in transit.	I.D.AM Assess Management ID.RA Risk Assessment ID.RM Risk Management Strategy PR.AC Identity Management and Access Control PR.AT Awareness and Training	USA Patriot Critical Infrastructure FIPS 140-3 Cryptographic module OMB A-130 Information Security FIPS 200 High Impact System

(continued)

Table 2-2. (*continued*)

Risk ID	Risk title	Risk mitigation strategy	CSF category ID	Security controls
013	Cloud assets	Have the virtual private network policy align with NIST 800-144 Guidelines on Security and Privacy in Public Cloud Computing.	ID.AM Asset Management ID.BE Business Environment PR.DS Data Security PR.MA Maintenance DE.CM Security Continuous Monitoring DE. DP Detection Processes RS.CO Communication	NIST 800-144 Security and Privacy in Public Cloud Computing OMB A-130 CNSSI 4009 Audit/ Audit log

(*continued*)

Table 2-2. (*continued*)

Risk ID	Risk title	Risk mitigation strategy	CSF category ID	Security controls
014	Telecommunications	Implement layers of assessment management and security controls with your policy. This will require compliance, awareness training, and vendor assessments for risk management.	ID.AM Assessment Management PR. IP Information Protection Processes and Procedures PR.PT Protective Technology DE. DP Protection Processes RS. RP Response Planning RS. CO Communications RS.AN Analysis RS.MI Mitigation RC.RP Recovery Planning	FIPS 201-2 access control OMB A-130 adequate security CNSSI 4009 audit FIPS 200 authentication OMB M-17-12 breach/environment of operation. FISMA confidentiality CNSSI 4009 cyberspace.
015	Physical	Install surveillance systems to retrieve digital footage of daily activities internally and externally, within civil rights. Increase access security methods relying on access key cards and identification cards.	ID.BE Business Environment ID.RA Risk Assessment PR.AC Identity Management and Access Control PR.AT Awareness and Training PR.PT Protective Technology	CNSSI 4009 boundary FIPS Authentication CNSSI 4009 Audit OMB a-130 authorization boundary OMB M-17-12 breach FIPS Countermeasures SP-800-63-3 Credential

The business cases Berkshire Hathaway must plan for includes business problems or opportunities, benefits, risks, technical solutions, timescales, and impacts on operations. Your organization will have a similar business case outline. Learning how to develop your organization's business cases should be simple but also must meet the needs of your assessment. To help define a clearly conveyed list of business cases, I have provided mitigation recommendations for each business case associated with Berkshire Hathaway based on this research. Keep in mind that any publicized security breach released into the media can create reputational damage and impact consumers' trust in the services and brand. Thus, implementing an effective reputational damage planning method will increase communication with personnel who are responsible for securing your organization's information assets. Also, this information will help improve the awareness training development that is essential for supporting the organization in educating personnel on what is required of them to comply with the organization's security policy that is implemented to control and prohibit access to authorized systems both internally and externally. Benefits include low civil liabilities, decrease in noncompliance regulatory fees and litigation costs, increased trust by consumers in the organization's brand name, cost savings, and security. The risk woven into each tier of business (i.e., physical, communication, security, technology tools, and personnel) is minimized. Thus, being aware of the technology tools' risks and how they can be easily compromised and infiltrated by unauthorized attack agents seeking to sabotage and vandalize the organization's web interface, business communications, technology assets (including hardware, software, internet, WIFI, information systems, and cloud computing architecture) will increase your ability to improve risk factors, implement better mitigation strategies, and increase your staff's knowledge compliance with your organization's policies.

In fact, aligning Berkshire Hathaway's business practices with an effective security policy that encompass risk assessment, risk management, infrastructure security procedures and planning, methods and strategies of communication, identifying management and access control, maintenance, security continuous monitoring methods and strategies, detection processes, response planning, methods of analysis and mitigation, and recovery planning is essential to managing the security risk associated with risk titles listed in the Risk Mitigation Strategy Security Controls Profile I created for Berkshire Hathaway. Your organization's risk mitigation strategy security controls profile will be similar. However, it is your duty of care to ensure you have developed a clear outline of the risks that require mitigation strategies, in order to ensure that the security risk mitigation approach relied on is effective. Implementing an effective security policy that aligns with these recommendations and guidelines should commence immediately and be audited quarterly, or as often as needed. Developing a plan for implementation should include steps offered in the "National Initiative for Cybersecurity in the Workplace Education" publication. This guideline supports the needs of the enterprise in achieving a risk assessment strategy that decreases potential risk associated with key components previously discussed (i.e., risk management, infrastructure security procedures and planning, identity management and access control, maintenance, security continuous monitoring, detection processes, response planning, analysis, mitigation, and recovery planning). Implementing a policy that outlines repercussions for noncompliance will help your personnel improve their adoption of such policy and align business operations with the security needs of the organization. In fact, Table 2-3 provides an Information Sensitivity Risk Profile that outlines the category of information you desire to secure, a description of the information assets, the level of sensitivity associated with this information, a description of how this information is used or processed, and a description of the IT assets usage and how such assets are stored.

Table 2-3. *Information Sensitivity Risk Profile*

Category of information	Description of the information asset(s)	Sensitivity of the information	How is this information used or processed?	IT assets using or storing this information
Customer records	Name, address, birthdate, driver's license, banking routing information	Strict confidentiality	To process orders, fulfill service obligations, maintain records, process payments	Computers (desktops/laptops), servers, cloud VPCs, physical filing systems, external hard drive storage, software
Trademarks	Brand logos and designs	Confidentiality	Legal ownership, liability suits	External hard drives, cloud VPNs, computers (desktops/laptops)

(continued)

Table 2-3. (*continued*)

Category of information	Description of the information asset(s)	Sensitivity of the information	How is this information used or processed?	IT assets using or storing this information
Patents	Models and methods of product development/service development	Confidentiality	Registered with federal court systems and state legal systems to identify brand products or services	External hard drives, software, computers (desktops/laptops), servers, cloud VPCs
Employee records	Name, salary, birthdate, banking direct deposit details, investment information, stock details, 401K, health and medical insurance	Confidentiality	Manages employee's records for salary, company investments, and liability insurance.	External hard drives, CRM software, computers (desktops/laptops), servers, and cloud VPCs
Vendor and third-party records	Name, contact person, address, phone number, payment details, and bank information	Confidentiality	Utilized to maintain records of consumers' credit card information and bank information	External hard drives, software, USB drives, computers (desktops/laptops), servers, and cloud VPCs
Software assets	Customer names, order numbers, tracking numbers, item numbers, credit card information, passwords, shipping address details	Strict confidentiality	Develops, transmits, and stores data files, order numbers, tracking information, backup, and archiving details	Internal software, USB drives, desktops/laptops

(*continued*)

Table 2-3. (*continued*)

Category of information	Description of the information asset(s)	Sensitivity of the information	How is this information used or processed?	IT assets using or storing this information
Hardware assets	System backup and archive, storage files, RAM	Strict confidentiality	Transmits data files internally and externally	Desktops/laptops, servers, networks, WIFI, and the Internet
Information systems assets	Product files, customer files, business transactions, payroll, and CRM	Strict confidentiality	Stores, transmits, and secures data files internally and externally	Telecommunication, WIFI, the Internet, servers, and networks.
Cloud assets	VPN, servers, IAM, and machine learning	Strict confidentiality	Stores and transmit data files securely	Server, network, key pairs
Physical security assets	Entrance access cards, biometric, printers, fax machines, supplies, desktop monitors, desktop computers, and laptops.	Strict confidentiality	Protects employees, Human Resource offices and cubes, plus company supplies and internal sensitive data resources	Entrance doors into the physical office

The risks listed in this profile are extensive and the risks listed for your organization will probably be just as extensive. Thus, it is important that you make sure to focus on each important and valued information and technology asset that enables your organization to achieve its goals, mission, and vision, while also achieving a return on investment. This is crucial to the success of your organization's lifecycle. Neglecting to do a thorough job adopting and establishing a clearly written Information Security Risk Profile can be costly in the long run. Making sure your organization updates this profile as needed will also enable you to stay current in trends of information security risk and enable you to know what method and strategies are important to deploy to safeguard your information assets from being targeted and successfully exploited. Table 2-4 shows clearly conveyed security profile risks. The highlighted color chart designates risks from high to low. It is important to be aware of the level of risk for your organization's security.

Table 2-4. *Security Profile Risk*

High Risk

Medium Risk

Low Risk

Risk ID	Risk Title	Description	Risk Category	Impact Level
001	Information extortion	Ransomware deployed to retrieve information assets via known vulnerable technology tools. Berkshire Hathaway, Inc. reports that terrorist acts can hinder their business operations. [6]	EXTREMELY HIGH	Catastrophic
002	Human error of failure	Employees accidently open an embedded link in an email sent from a known person, who is not the actual sender. This is considered spoofing. Berkshire Hathaway, Inc. reports they need qualified personnel to operate their businesses. [7]	HIGH	Medium
003	Compromise of intellectual property	External attackers gain access to the network via a known vulnerability and retrieves data files from an unsecure computer device.	Medium	Moderate
004	Technical hardware failures or installation errors	Hardware lacks required updates and enables attackers to gain access to the computer, network, information systems, cloud, or IT. Berkshire Hathaway, Inc. classifies this as Cybersecurity attack risk. [8]	HIGH	Catastrophic
005	Technical software failures or installation errors	Software applications installed are infused with known vulnerabilities that can impede on security vulnerabilities woven in the current information system, network, hardware, cloud infrastructure, and mobile or WIFI. Berkshire Hathaway, Inc. considers these risks as cybersecurity issues.	HIGH	Medium

(continued)

Table 2-4. (*continued*)

006	Technological obsolescence	Products or services are no longer required and replaced with new versions.	HIGH	Medium
007	Sabotage or vandalism	Former employees wreak havoc on the external and internal landscape of the enterprise and destroy USB drives, cut cords, and write negative reports online.	Medium	Low
008	Forces of nature	Tornadoes, Power outages, Hurricane, Floods, and Windstorms. Berkshire Hathaway, Inc. lists this as a climate change issue. [9]	Medium	Low
009	Theft	Employees steal computers, USB drives, monitors, mobile devices, files, customer data, account numbers, etc.	Medium	Medium
010	Software attacks	Application programming interfaces are installed with known vulnerabilities that exploit the business and share private information.	HIGH	Catastrophic
011	Vendor & Third-party records	Files of vendor names, addresses, and account numbers can be stolen and sold for monetary gain.	Medium	Low
012	Information system assets	Retrieval of employee's names, addresses, salary, and bank routing numbers can be used for malicious purposes.	HIGH	Catastrophic
013	Cloud assets	Retrieval of sensitive enterprise data, i.e., Stocks, banking accounts, and financial transactions as well as enterprise information system assets, including passwords and multifactor authentication data.	HIGH	Medium
014	Telecommunications	Communication channels targeted for covert surveillance include everything from phone lines and online chat to mobile phone data.	HIGH	Medium
015	Physical	Entrance access cards, biometric, printer, fax machine, supplies, and desktop monitors, desktop computers, and laptops each can be hacked, stolen, or manipulated to enable cyberattacks or other forms of sabotage. Berkshire Hathaway, Inc. lists this with property and casualty insurance loss. [10]	HIGH	Medium

The level of risk associated with each category of information conveys the level of security that should be implemented to ensure that effective mitigation methods and strategies are deployed to secure these assets. Neglecting to secure these assets will impact the organization economically and reputationally. Thus, it's essential for Berkshire Hathaway and your organization to rely on and use the NIST 800 publication series. These recommendations and guidelines can help you increase security control and risk management strategies to protect private sector information systems, technology, and the cloud from unauthorized intrusion and cyberattacks. Aligning your organization's security, information assets, information technology, cloud, and all technology tools usage policy with the recommendations and guidelines of the NIST SP 800 series publications, will integrate a regulatory system that demands compliance. When personnel neglect to adhere to these policies, it is your organization's responsibility to respond with a stern approach to improve noncompliance with policies. Failing to do so will result in a continued lifecycle of noncompliance that will cost the organization tremendously.

Case Study

Policy compliance and risk factors go hand in hand. When the customer service representatives (CSR) retrieve personal information from clients, they create a record that identifies name, address, city, state, ZIP code, credit card information, bank routing numbers for checking and saving accounts as well as numbers for each vehicle they own when applying for insurance offered by Berkshire Hathaway. Each CSR operates individually, so it is impossible to determine which CSR will be the vulnerability to the organization's secure information system.

Let's say a customer calls and starts answering each question the CSR is required to ask. The telecommunication service provider (i.e., Cox Communications) used for each phone call has known vulnerabilities that cybercriminals can use to gain access and intercept communication with the router to obtain passwords as well as expose web activity that returns the user's call log without origin or permission checks. This enables a cybercriminal to inject a JavaScript payload that runs in a browser or app without user interaction or consent, which also enables the attacker to send the user's call logs to a remote server via an XML HTTP request or Fetch. [11]

What can be done to prevent this from happening? What should the IT practitioner do to patch this problem? Who should the IT practitioner contact to gain support in preventing any of the known vulnerabilities woven into the telecommunication systems from being targeted by unauthorized users?

Berkshire Hathaway must stay aware of the vulnerabilities integrated in the telecommunication systems relied on as well as the peripherals used that are common entrance points for cyberattacks. Is the IT practitioner aware of how to research the CVE website and search for known vulnerabilities woven within every technology tool used? Is the IT practitioner effective in their approach to implementing effective information assurance risk management strategies? How can Berkshire Hathaway be sure that any hired IT practitioner is aware of the known vulnerabilities in any technology tool relied on for business operations and communication?

Summary

Neglecting to upgrade your organization's technology risk management and analysis strategies with the recommendations in this chapter can impact how successful your organization manages the risk associated with the technology tools and information assets it owns and utilizes for business communication and operations. Taking time to outline the known risk factors and categorize these risk factors and to determine the level of impact each risk factor embodies, helps you improve the scale of security and risk mitigation strategies for your organization. Having this clarity enables you to effectively present these details to executives, stakeholders, and personnel who lack the clarity needed to understand why increasing information systems, technology, and cloud budgets is necessary to implement effective training and increase security. Neglecting to be diligent in defining clearly conveyed profile charts will create a gateway for successful cyberattacks and cyberincidents, which will impact cost and possibly result in reputational damage. These guidelines will help your organization improve its weaknesses and build opportunities to upgrade the system where needed, while staying current with trends in security features that meet the needs of each tier of technology implemented.

Discussion Questions

1. What is NIST 800-53?

2. What is the National Cybersecurity Workplace Framework?

3. What are five risk factors listed in the risk factor profile for Berkshire Hathaway?

4. Why should you provide a description of the risk factors listed in your organization's risk factor chart?

5. Why should you create a risk mitigation strategy security control profile?

6. What type of security controls can help prepare your organization to protect its assets?

7. What information should be included in your organization's Information Sensitivity Risk Profile?

8. Why is a security profile risk table important for your organization?

Keywords

information extortion, technology obsolescence, information asset, risk management, mitigation strategies, and identity management

CHAPTER 3

Policy Compliance Strategies

Coded passage

Learning objectives:

- Understand how to assess all privacy issues relating to your organization.

- Understand how to assess, develop, and manage a privacy compliance risk profile.

- Understand how to assess, develop, and manage a privacy compliance controls profile.

- Understand how to assess, develop, and manage a privacy compliance risk mitigation strategy.

© Bradley Fowler 2023
B. Fowler, *Information Assurance and Risk Management Strategies*,
https://doi.org/10.1007/978-1-4842-9742-1_3

The knowledge and information provided in Chapters 1 and 2 enables you to understand how the information assurance strategies implemented on behalf of Berkshire Hathaway can be applied to your organization. Modifying the details and using the tables to help how you perform risk assessments and management strategies will help you tremendously! You also learned how simple it is to research a Fortune 500 corporation. Using the open-source database of DandB.com, I was able to compile information about how Berkshire Hathaway represents itself to investors and shareholders compared to how it presents itself on its customer website interface. Additionally, I acquired information from Berkshire Hathaway's Form 10-K Annual Report, presenting information about the company honestly to its investors and shareholders regarding the current cybersecurity risk factors. In addition, I gained information about Berkshire Hathaway's services and history as conveyed in the Hoovers profile. This information enabled me to comprehend the corporation and its geopolitical environment as well as who its customers are, what the corporation sells, and how it makes revenue. Then I provided you with details about the laws and policies to which the corporation is held accountable and shared details about the corporation's information assets, subsystem and software assets, hardware assets, and how such assets are utilized to conduct business operations. Furthermore, I shared a well conveyed Information Profile chart identifying categories of information requiring intense security against loss of confidentiality, integrity, and availability, which are key components of the CIA triad. Moreover, I introduced you to 10 distinct categories of information, including category of information, description of the information assets, sensitivity of the information, how this information is used or processed, the IT assets used for storing sensitive information, hardware assets, software assets, information system security assets, network component assets, and people assets. I also shared research conveying the types of information Berkshire Hathaway collects, processes, transmit, and stores as a part of its business operations. Lastly, I reported the type of information technology and systems Berkshire Hathaway utilizes to accomplish business objectives.

In this chapter, I share another analysis that focuses on the privacy issues that currently impact Berkshire Hathaway, which includes 10 privacy issues I identified from additional research. For each issue, I present an analysis that explains why these issues are important for Berkshire Hathaway, and I discuss the legal and policy drivers that make these issues important. Furthermore, I report the non-compliance risks associated with three of these issues and provide another analysis regarding the privacy compliance risk profile that presents privacy-related compliance risks. In fact, to help you better understand the issues, I share an introductory paragraph explaining the relationship between the previously identified privacy issues and the privacy compliance risks profile. This includes providing details regarding the type of information presented in Table 3-1. I also describe the process and documents utilized to construct the Privacy Compliance Risk Profile in Table 3-1. I share a Privacy Compliance Control Profile that provides an introductory paragraph explaining the privacy compliance controls profile, and describe the process and documents utilized to construct the Privacy Compliance Control Profile that delivers 10 rows positioned in Table 3-2.

Then I present a separate section titled "Privacy Compliance Risk Mitigation Strategy" that represents a high-level strategy for implementing risk mitigation (security controls), which were presented previously in Chapters 1 and 2. Finally, I share recommendations and conclusions, including a summary of the information contained in Chapters 1 and 2 and a summary regarding the business needs and business benefits that support implementing the Privacy Compliance Risk Mitigation Strategy and the allocation of resources by Berkshire Hathaway.

Who Is Berkshire Hathaway?

Berkshire Hathaway Inc. ("Berkshire," "Company," or "Registrant") is a holding company that owns subsidiaries engaged in numerous diverse business activities. The most important of these are insurance businesses conducted on both a primary basis and a reinsurance basis, a freight rail transportation business, and a group of utility and energy generation and distribution businesses. Berkshire Hathaway also owns and operates numerous other businesses engaged in a variety of manufacturing, services, retailing. and other activities. Berkshire Hathaway is domiciled in the state of Delaware, and its corporate headquarters is in Omaha, Nebraska. [1] To manage information, Berkshire Hathaway relies on information security as a method to protect sensitive information assets belonging to it and its subsidiaries. Berkshire Hathaway's total corporate family membership includes 6521 company names. [2] Each headquarter location hosts sensitive data on the corporation's information system, including data stored or transmitted via virtual servers, leased or owned. Information hosted on these information systems includes names, client lists, addresses, phone numbers, email addresses, email responses, internet search history, documents containing names and account numbers, information regarding trademark secrets, intellectual property, financial resources, and deeds of properties. In addition, details convey that Berkshire

Hathaway relies on email to conduct daily business transactions that report sensitive information. The in-office WIFI is enabled to support the usage of the Internet to transmit documents across a public or private cloud, which is hosted by a third-party service provider. Each employee connected to one of the 6521 company names listed on the D & B Hoover website interface utilizes the corporation's network, including the LAN, WAN, and WLAN. The LAN, WAN, and WLAN can become entrance points for unauthorized system intrusion. For instance, across a wireless LAN, intruders can deploy an attack against the wireless client in a peer-to-peer approach. This attack method can enable the intruder to gain network access using a legitimate client as an accepted entry point. [3] Vulnerabilities embedded in the WAN are entrance points that enable hackers to redirect traffic and shut down vulnerable networks. [4]

Any fax machine connected to the WIFI to help support transmission of data both receiving and sending can be another entrance point for a successful cyberattack. In fact, research presented by Charlie Osborn on ZDNet explains that fax machines are commonly relied on by businesses and a communication protocol vulnerability is woven into them, leaving these technology tools exposed to cyberattacks. [5] Furthermore, Osborn conveys that fax numbers provide an open access point. When cybercriminals gain access to fax numbers, they can send malicious image files to victims. [6]

Printers can also provide entrance points for cyberattacks. Any device connected to a network that is improperly managed and incorrectly configured will expose sensitive information to unauthorized individuals who can exploit and misuse whatever information attained. [7] The WIFI creates a vulnerability because recent reports explain these tools are security risk. In fact, Howard Solomon reported that small business administrators utilizing Cisco routers were at risk for website redirects and more. [8] Solomon also shared that many vulnerabilities enable remote attackers to deploy DoS attacks and/or gain access to devices to deploy horrible malicious acts. In fact, it is publicly reported on the D & B Hoover website that Berkshire Hathaway utilizes Cisco routers; these routers embody known vulnerabilities and threats. Understanding the known vulnerabilities and threats associated with every device and technology tool, software, and hardware application your organization utilizes for business operations and communication can better prepare you to improve information assurance through effective cybersecurity methods and information assurance risk management strategies.

As an ISTC practitioner, you should be aware that these risk factors are discussed in the 800 Special Publication series published by the National Institute of Standards and Technology, both 800-53 and 800-37. NIST SP-800-53 provides recommendations and guidelines to assess and mitigate security and privacy matters, including privacy controls for information systems and organizations to protect organizational operations and assets, individuals, other organizations, and the nation from a diverse set of threats and risks, including hostile attacks, human errors, natural disasters, structural failures, foreign intelligence entities, and privacy risks. The controls are flexible and customizable and implemented as part of an organization-wide process to manage risk. [9] Additionally, NIST-SP-800-37 was developed and introduced to enable practitioners to effectively deploy disciplined, structured, and flexible processes for managing security and privacy risks, including risk control for information security categorization as well as control selection, implementation, assessment, system and common control authorizations, and continuous monitoring. [10]

Privacy Issues Impacting Berkshire Hathaway

According to the United States Security Exchange Commission, Berkshire Hathaway Form 10-K published in December 2021, Berkshire Hathaway reported that its subsidiaries are vulnerable to certain risks. [11] These vulnerabilities create risks and uncertainties. Berkshire Hathaway also reported that general business risks encompass terrorist acts and cyberattacks. Because Berkshire Hathaway and its 6521 subsidiaries engage with consumers and collect, store, and transmit information assets belonging to consumers, domestically and internationally, it is held accountable under federal and state laws as well as EU laws regarding privacy of the information assets it collects, stores, and transmits via the Internet regarding consumer names, addresses, phone numbers, bank routing and account numbers, credit card information, and additional sensitive information assets. Thus, the 10 known privacy issues Berkshire Hathaway commonly must be aware of include

- Collection of sensitive information

- Retention of data collected

- Logging of data collected and stored

- Generation of data

- Transformation of data for business usage

- Use of consumer information

- Disclosure of consumer information and privacy of information

- Sharing of consumer information with third parties

- Transmission of consumer information across the Internet and WIFI

- Disposal of information

Known privacy issues associated with each of these 10 information assets, requires immediate security and assessment actions to ensure that Berkshire Hathaway is compliant with federal, state, and EU laws and policies enacted to protect the personal information of consumers and to decrease fraud and misuse of the data collected. Therefore, the collection of sensitive information must be retained, logged, generated, transformed, utilized, disclosed, shared, transmitted, and disposed of in alignment with **global policies**, regulations, and laws. For instance, some of the laws that Berkshire Hathaway must adhere to include the Children's Online Privacy Protection Act, the California Online Privacy Protection Act including the Do Not Track amendment, the EU General Data Protection Regulation (GDPR), the EU Cookies Directive, and the Personal Information Protection and Electronics Documents Act. Three non-compliance risks associated with these issues include reputational damage to products, services, and the corporate brand, economic loss, and embarrassment.

Privacy Compliance Risks Profile

Previously reported privacy issues correlating with the Privacy Compliance Risk Profile are defined by cybersecurity risk factors reported by Berkshire Hathaway in its 2021 U.S. Security and Exchange Commission 10-K form. Presented in Table 3-1, the Privacy Compliance Risk Profile offers details about privacy compliance risk issues Berkshire Hathaway faces as well as the risk categories and the impact level of each risk. These issues are the focus of this risk profile because Berkshire Hathaway reported these general business risks (i.e., computer viruses, malicious code, unauthorized access, phishing efforts, DoS attacks, disruption and failure of technology services, safety failures, regulatory compliance failures, and the inability to protect information assets against unauthorized users, loss of assets, exposure of critical information as well as reputational damage) in its Form 10-K. Your organization may share the same concerns or similar issues. However, it is important to focus on defining a Privacy Compliance Risk Profile that correctly aligns with your organization to assure your risk mitigation strategies are effective.

Table 3-1. *Privacy Compliance Risk Profile*

Risk ID	Privacy risk title	Description	Risk category	Impact level
001	Computer viruses	Can create an ease of access to Berkshire Hathaway's information systems and enable deployment of attack vectors to exploit the systems [NIST-SP-800-53]	People	High
002	Malicious code	Can impact the security of information systems and information technology relied on for storage, transmission, and development of data [NIST-SP-800-39]	People	High
003	Unauthorized access	Requires assessing who should have access and who should not [NIST-SP-800-37 and GDPR]	People	Medium
004	Phishing efforts	Enables social engineering of information systems and email accounts to be infused with malware [NIST SP-800-53 and GDPR]	Computers, software	High
005	Denial-of-service attacks	Enables attack methods that flood web interfaces and interrupt virtual business operations [NIST SP-800-53]	People	High
006	Disruption and failure of technology services	Impacts the daily business operations and can create reputational damage [NIST-SP-800-37]	Computers, software	High
007	Safety failures	Planned safety procedures fail to meet the demands and needs of the enterprise. [NIST-SP-800-53]	People	Medium
008	Regulatory compliance failures	Personnel neglects to adhere to regulatory and policy. [NIST-SP-800-53, NIST-SP-800-181 and GDPR]	People	High

(*continued*)

Table 3-1. (*continued*)

Risk ID	Privacy risk title	Description	Risk category	Impact level
009	Inability to protect information assets	Planned procedures and strategies do not provide security effectively. [NIST-SP-800-53, NIST-SP-800-181, and GDPR]	People	Medium
010	Reputational damage	Public becomes knowledgeable of business security issues and failures and thus stops trusting the services provided. [NIST-SP-800-53 and GDPR]	People	Medium

The Privacy Compliance Risk Plan for each of these privacy risk issues aligns with the procedures, recommendations, and guidelines defined by each NIST Special Publication 800 series, as well as the ISO/IEC 27000 series. ISO 27001:2013 provides specifications for the assessment of performance within an information security management system (ISMS). Organizations that comply with the standardizations gain an official certification provided by an independent and accredited certification committee on successful completion of a formal audit process. [12] Thus, implementing clearly conveyed security policies must be the next step in defining a security plan to enforce compliance to improve the corporation's security strategies. In fact, security policies must include corporate policies, security, and supporting policies. Any method you implement should mirror the process of policy development, connectivity, and implementation (Figure 3-1).

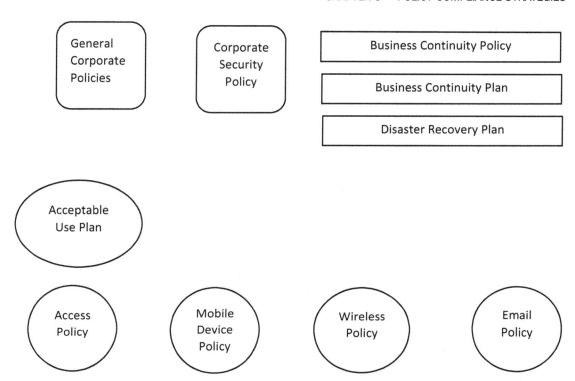

Figure 3-1. *Security policy process*

Relying on NIST SP 800 Series publications and aligning all practitioner practices and procedures with the recommendations and guidelines woven in the content of (ISC)[2] Systems Security Certified Practitioner Official Study Guide can provide a clear understanding of the methods, strategies, regulations, policies, and laws you should adhere to and understand to help support the security and privacy needs of your organization. Furthermore, you must effectively assess the laws and policies enacted by the European Union and its newly enacted General Data Protection Regulation (GDPR). Doing so can decrease liabilities that will arise from non-compliance, especially when there are system failures and security breaches that result in the loss of data stored on information technology, information systems, and the cloud. Regardless of who was responsible for the security breach, your organization is responsible for informing all clients about the breach as well as the U.S. Federal Bureau of Investigation.

Privacy Compliance Controls Profile

The privacy compliance control profile I created for Berkshire Hathaway in Table 3-2 was completed with details reported in Berkshire Hathaway's U.S. Security and Exchange Commission 10-K Form published in December 2021. In the 10-K Form, the general business risks includes terrorist acts, which can impact business operations as well as invoke cybersecurity risks. Thus, it is determined that these privacy compliance controls are beneficial in supporting the needs of the corporation and its security concerns. The policies listed derive from NIST SP-800-53, Rev.5, which was amended in 2020. I also listed the extended policies for each separate security control. Thus, it is recommended Berkshire Hathaway assess these NIST policies and make necessary updates to the current information system, information technology, information security, cloud, and additional policies developed, implemented, and relied on for security controls to assure alignment with federal, state, and EU laws. Otherwise, Berkshire Hathaway risks reputational damage, civil liabilities, and criminal prosecution. In Chapter 6, I provide an extensive outline of policy templates that can be utilized and modified to meet the needs of any organization. Of course, your organization will have similar privacy compliance control profile risk titles. However, these security controls are international and can easily align with your organization's privacy compliance control profile. Using this approach can be beneficial for your organization, especially when applied as presented in this privacy compliance control profile in Table 3-2.

Table 3-2. *Privacy Compliance Control Profile*

Risk ID	Risk title	Compliance risk mitigation strategy	NIST security controls
001	Computer viruses	Configuration management will implement effective system updates that help assess potential risks in software utilized for enterprise computer systems, including information technology, information systems, and cloud infrastructure.	CM-1 [Policy & Procedures] CM-2 [Baseline Configuration] CM-3 [Configuration Change Control] CM-4 [Impact Analysis] CM-8 [System Component Inventory] CM-10 [Software Usage Restrictions] CM-11 [User Installed Software]. These security controls are encapsulated in NIST-800-53 Rev.5, see Notes [1] below.

(*continued*)

Table 3-2. (*continued*)

Risk ID	Risk title	Compliance risk mitigation strategy	NIST security controls
002	Malicious code	Implementing effective software assessment plans and strategies will decrease the risks associated with reliance on malicious code embedded within software utilized for information systems, information technology, and cloud infrastructures. It is recommended to always search the CVE.mitre.org website for updates on malicious code issues with all software utilized. See Notes [2] below.	SI-3 [Malicious Code Protection] RA-1 [Policy & Procedures] RA-3 [Risk Assessment] RA-5 [Vulnerability Monitoring and Scanning] RA-7 [Risk Response] RA-8 [Privacy Impact Assessment] RA-9 [Criticality Analysis] RA-10 [Threat Hunting] These security controls are woven in NIST-SP-800-53 Rev.5, see Notes [3] below.

(*continued*)

Table 3-2. (*continued*)

Risk ID	Risk title	Compliance risk mitigation strategy	NIST security controls
003	Unauthorized access	Developing a policy that prevents access to databases and information assets of value to the ongoing business operations and monetary growth of the enterprise should define who should have access and how access control should be granted and monitored.	AC-1 [Policy and Procedures] AC-2 [Account Management] AC-3 [Access Enforcement] AC-4 [Information Flow Enforcement] AC-6 [Less Privilege] AC-11 [Device Lock] AC-13 [Supervise and Review-Access Control] AC-16 [Security and Privacy Attributes] AC-24 [Access Control Decisions] These security controls are woven in NIST-SP-800-53, Rev.5; see Notes [4] below.

(*continued*)

Table 3-2. (*continued*)

Risk ID	Risk title	Compliance risk mitigation strategy	NIST security controls
004	Phishing efforts	Increasing personnel awareness training to decrease the number of successful phishing attacks will help support any implemented mitigation strategy.	AT-1 [Policy & Procedures] AT-2 [Literacy Training and Awareness] AT-3 [Role-based Training] AT-4 [Training Records] AT-6 [Training Feedback] These security controls are woven in NIST-SP-800-53 Rev.5, see Notes [5] below.
005	Denial-of-service attacks	Implementing effective Security Socket Layers on web pages and implementing effective risk management controls that include firewalls and intrusion detection can be instrumental in controlling successful attacks against enterprise web interfaces.	SI-1 [Policy & Procedures] SI-3 [Malicious Code Protection] SI-4 [System Monitoring] SI-6 [Security and Privacy Function Verification] These security controls are woven in NIST-SP-800-53 Rev.5; see Notes [6] below.

(*continued*)

Table 3-2. (*continued*)

Risk ID	Risk title	Compliance risk mitigation strategy	NIST security controls
006	Disruption and failure of technology services	Defining a policy that requires the backup of all information systems can be instrumental in helping combat technology failures as well as implementing generators and policies that govern usage and security of these technology tool support systems.	SI-4 [System Monitoring] SI-1 [Policy & Procedures] CA-1 [Policy & Procedures] CA-5 [Plan of Action & Milestone] CA-7 [Continuous Monitoring] CA-9 [Internal System Connections] These controls are rendered in NIST-SP-800-53, Rev.5; see Notes [7] below.

(*continued*)

Table 3-2. (*continued*)

Risk ID	Risk title	Compliance risk mitigation strategy	NIST security controls
007	Safety failures	Defining safety policies and procedures for upgrading and testing safety policies for failures prior to an incident can help decrease this issue.	IR-1 [Policy & Procedures] IR-2 [Incident Response & Training] IR-4 [Incident Handling] IR-6 [Incident Reporting] IR-7 [Incident Response Assistance] AU-1 [Policy & Procedures] AU-2 [Event Logging] AU-4 [Audit Log Storage Capacity] AU-9 [Protection of Audit Information] MA-1 [Policy & Procedures] MA-2 [Controlled Maintenance] MA-3 [Maintenance Tools] These security controls derive from NIST-SP-800-53. Rev.5; see Notes [8], [9], [10] below.

(*continued*)

Table 3-2. (*continued*)

Risk ID	Risk title	Compliance risk mitigation strategy	NIST security controls
008	Regulatory compliance failures	Maintaining an up-to-date regulatory compliance policy, personnel awareness training, and auditing personnel awareness training is useful in preventing regulatory compliance failure.	PS-1 [Policy & Procedures] PS-7 [External Personnel Security] SC-1 [Policy & Procedures] SC-2 [Separation of System and User Functionality] These security controls were woven into NIST-SP-800-53, Rev.5, see Notes [11] & [12] below.
009	Inability to protect information assets	Reinforcing an effectively developed policy that requires auditing of information systems hosting information assets should be mandatory and updated as needed annually.	AC-Access Control AU-Audit and Accountability CP-Contingency Planning MA-Maintenance PM-Program Management PS-Personnel Security RA-Risk Assessment SI-System and Information Integrity

(*continued*)

Table 3-2. (*continued*)

Risk ID	Risk title	Compliance risk mitigation strategy	NIST security controls
010	Reputational damage	Managing all information systems, information technologies, and usage of cloud services, platforms, and infrastructure will help decrease security issues that can result in reputational damage.	PM-Program Management PL-Planning IA-Identification and Authentication

Notes:

[1] NIST.gov (2022). CPRT/ 800-53/ CM. Retrieved from Cybersecurity and Privacy Reference Tool | CSRC (nist.gov)

[2] CVE.mitre.org (2022) `https://cwe.mitre.org/data/definitions/506.html`

[3] NIST.gov (2022). CPRT/800-53/RA. Retrieved from Cybersecurity and Privacy Reference Tool | CSRC (nist.gov)

[4] NIST.gov (2022). CPRT/800-53/AC. Retrieved from Cybersecurity and Privacy Reference Tool | CSRC (nist.gov)

[5] NIST.gov (2022). CPRT/800-53/AT. Retrieved from Cybersecurity and Privacy Reference Tool | CSRC (nist.gov)

[6] Nist.gov (2022). CPRT/800-53/SI. Retrieved from Cybersecurity and Privacy Reference Tool | CSRC (nist.gov)

[7] Nist.gov (2022). CPRT/800-53/CA. Retrieved from Cybersecurity and Privacy Reference Tool | CSRC (nist.gov)

[8] Nist.gov (2022). CPRT/800-53/IR. Retrieved from Cybersecurity and Privacy Reference Tool | CSRC (nist.gov)

[9] Nist.gov (2022). CPRT/800-53/AU. Retrieved from Cybersecurity and Privacy Reference Tool | CSRC (nist.gov)

[10] Nist.gov (2022). CPRT/800-53/MA. Retrieved from Cybersecurity and Privacy Reference Tool | CSRC (nist.gov)

[11] Nist.gov (2022). CPRT/800-53/PS. Retrieved from Cybersecurity and Privacy Reference Tool | CSRC (nist.gov)

[12] Nist.gov (2022). CPRT/800-53/SC. Retrieved from Cybersecurity and Privacy Reference Tool | CSRC (nist.gov)

Privacy Compliance Risk Mitigation Strategy

In this section, I provide a summary of Berkshire Hathaway's business risks as reported in the U.S. Securities and Exchange Commission 10-K form, published December 2021. Berkshire Hathaway reported that the threats to business operations commonly include computer viruses, malicious code, unauthorized access, phishing efforts, DoS attacks, disruption and failure of technology services, safety failures, regulatory compliance failures, and an inability to protect information assets against unauthorized users, loss of assets, exposure of critical information as well as reputational damage. When Berkshire Hathaway willfully adheres and aligns with the recommendations and guidelines provided by the National Institute of Standards and Technology policies and the European Commission enacted General Data Protection Regulation, this will help secure information assets, information technology, information systems, and cloud services, infrastructures, and platforms relied on by the 6521 subsidiaries owned and operated by Berkshire Hathaway. When you examine the publicly known threats and vulnerabilities your organization has with the current information system, information technology, and cloud, your profile table should mirror what has been deployed on behalf of Berkshire Hathaway.

One way to effectively assess threats woven and embedded in the technology tools relied on for business operations is by deploying a threat model. **Threat modeling** is about using models to find security problems. Using a model means abstracting away a lot of details to provide a look at a bigger picture, rather than the code itself. [13] Using a **diagram board** is a dynamic way to map out the technology tools used within the enterprise that require effective security methods, planning, and strategies to manage external and internal threats and vulnerabilities. Making a list of NIST policy recommendations that align with managing threats that impact information security is a second starting point. Your organization can build a list of **trust boundaries**, which are boundaries representing controls. Your organization's list should include accounts, network interfaces, additional physical computers, virtual machines, AI, cloud, and organizational boundaries. Next, you can assess external entities that may create threats to the organization and the technology tools and systems relied on. Additionally, you should focus attention on feasible threats. After all, four types of actions must be conducted to help protect your organization against each threat. [14] The first action is to **mitigate threats**, which requires implementing effective policy control and risk management assessments. The second action is to eliminate threats, which requires establishing authentication techniques that require personnel to have privileges to access detailed information or information systems and technology tools or compartments. Your organization should also consider the level of threats and possibly transfer any threats and risk associated with such. This requires establishing boundaries and limiting who, what, when, where, and how. Remember that NIST SP-800-53, 800-37, 800-181, and other NIST series publications are useful in managing the risks and threats associated with business systems defined by technology tools. Another approach to successfully managing these threats is to use threat modeling tools. **Bug tracking systems** are your first tool of reliance. Trike is one tool that can be useful; Sea Monster is another. Commercial tools include Threat Modeler, Corporate Threat Modeler, Secur/Tree, Little-JIL, and Microsoft's SDL Threat Modeling Tool. Keep in mind that these tools may be off the market and new tools may have been introduced. Conducting a search will help you discover useful tools to eliminate and control threats to your technology tools, information technology, information systems, and the cloud. Partnering with each software and hardware manufacturer and following their recommendations is crucial to managing the security of your organization's technology tools and assets.

Furthermore, make sure all methods of privacy compliance mitigation strategies deployed on behalf of your organization and the usage of business technology tools to render quality services and products align with the CIA triad of confidentiality, integrity, and availability. This is essential to staying compliant with federal, state, and EU policies, laws, and regulations that govern information technology, information systems, the cloud, software, hardware, and privacy of these technology environments and tools. Just as important is having a timeframe to deploy effective security audits and evaluations to help manage how effective implementation of policies will be and should be. This includes effectively developing and implementing awareness training programs that increase personnel's knowledge of their roles and responsibilities in protecting the information assets and technology tools and systems utilized to conduct business for your organization.

Recommendations and Conclusions

Berkshire Hathaway delivers customer services and products that help meet business and personal needs, including real estate, retail, railways, and utilities. Due to the continued collection and storage of consumer data, Berkshire Hathaway is required by federal law to protect consumer's data under the following:

- Communications Act

- Federal Privacy Act

- Electronic Communications Privacy Act

- Unlawful Access to Stored Communications

- Computer Fraud and Abuse Act

- National Information Infrastructure Protection Act

- Security and Freedom Through Encryption Act

- Digital Millennium Copyright Act

- National Cybersecurity Protection Act

Neglecting to align the information security policy with these acts can be costly if litigation is filed against Berkshire Hathaway for violating consumers' privacy. Thus, it is essential that Berkshire Hathaway develop, implement, and manage an effective approach to information security management. By doing so, Berkshire Hathaway decreases its chances of being sued and/or held liable for violating consumers' electronic communication sharing and data storage efforts. In fact, Berkshire Hathaway has a tremendous burden to protect and secure its information assets from cyberattacks, cyberterrorists, cyberhacktivists, cyberespionage, and cybercriminals. With the listed technologies in use conveyed on the D & B Hoover website, cybercriminals can exploit the known vulnerabilities integrated in each of the software applications Berkshire Hathaway's 6521 subsidiaries rely on. Thus, one effective approach to resolve this matter is to make sure the personnel responsible for managing these technology tools and systems are current with trends regarding the known vulnerabilities engulfed in each technology tool and system relied on, including information systems, information technology, the cloud, software, and hardware. They must also know how to effectively patch and mitigate each threat and vulnerability woven in these systems and technology tools.

Furthermore, those responsible for managing Berkshire Hathaway's technology tools and systems must be knowledgeable of their role in developing clearly conveyed written reports that include policy recommendations and guidelines enacted by the National Institute of Standards and Technology. Not only are those managing the technology tools and systems for Berkshire Hathaway held responsible and accountable, but so too are the personnel who access, utilize, store, and create documents and transmit information assets that drive the business operations for Berkshire Hathaway across the Internet and WIFI networks. They must be trained effectively to understand how to safeguard the information assets, information technology, information systems, cloud, hardware, software, and networks from threats and vulnerabilities. To increase compliance, Berkshire Hathaway must increase policies that force personnel to comply with the security plans to keep Berkshire Hathaway from being liable under federal, state, and EU laws, regulations, and policy.

To achieve this goal, Berkshire Hathaway must increase its professional representation of reliable and trained technology practitioners who can effectively demonstrate due diligence to deploy and implement recommended security methods and strategies that decrease vulnerabilities associated with each of the technology tools and systems in use. According to the U.S. Security and Exchange Commission Form 10-K issued December 2021, Berkshire Hathaway is knowledgeable of the risk it currently has and conveys to investors and shareholders that its cybersecurity risks may cause service interruptions, safety failures, security events, regulatory compliance failures, and an inability to protect information and assets against unauthorized users and other operational difficulties. The company also conveys that any attacks deployed against its systems will result in loss of assets and critical information and will expose it to remediation costs and reputational damage. [15]

Case Study

Traditionally, Berkshire Hathaway's ISTC practitioners have acquired educational and certification training for their role and responsibilities as ISTC practitioners through reputable and accredited learning institutions. Each learning program rendered a quality training program that should position each ISTC practitioner to effectively assess, develop, implement, manage, and secure all information systems, information technology, cloud services, infrastructure, or platforms utilized for business operations and communication. Yet, when any ISTC practitioner lacks efficient educational training and acquires the role and responsibility to safeguard an organization's information assets, that ISTC practitioner holds the power to protect the organization from harm.

However, when Berkshire Hathaway's ISTC practitioners fail to align policy and policy enforcement with the recommendations rendered by the National Institute of Standards and Technology Special Publication Series, the ISTC practitioner enables weaknesses to become threats, which leads to system vulnerabilities. Neglecting to understand NIST Special Publications that empower ISTC practitioners leaves Berkshire Hathaway susceptible to increased cybersecurity risk factors that are being ignored and this enables attackers to gain access. But if Berkshire Hathaway does not have an effective ISTC practitioner team managing its information systems, information technology, and cloud, who is accountable for the effective and efficient security of the organization's information assets? Who can inform stakeholders and executive leaders that a security breach occurred, honestly?

Without an effective team of ISTC practitioners, Berkshire Hathaway will remain victimizable and its assets will be open to misuse, not only by external threats but internal threats too. Who is to blame? How does this issue get resolved? Unless there is a continued effort to understand the known vulnerabilities integrated in every software application relied upon, Berkshire Hathaway cannot thwart and deter cyber incidents. Thus, the ISTC practitioner must step up and continue being trained, and also increase training of their workplace personnel. Otherwise, Berkshire Hathaway is wasting revenue on insufficient ISTC personnel.

Summary

Berkshire Hathaway must increase auditing all technology tools and systems relied upon for business needs and operations, quarterly or as needed, to ensure increased security is deployed against potential risks embedded within these systems and technology tools. This will require Berkshire Hathaway to hire qualified ISTC practitioners who understand the needs of the enterprise and its reliance on technology tools, including information systems, information technology, cloud, software, and hardware. Otherwise, the organization and its subsidiaries will remain vulnerable to victimization, which could result in reputational damage and impact consumer trust in the services and products rendered by Berkshire Hathaway.

In addition, neglecting to upgrade technology tools and systems relied upon as recommended by the manufacturers enables the organization to be victimized. After all, attack agents can acquire access through the vulnerabilities in each tier of technology, if effective security risk assessments are not deployed regularly to assess these technology tools and systems. Utilizing these guidelines will help your organization improve its weaknesses and upgrade the system where needed, while staying current with trends in security features to meet the needs of each tier of technology implemented and relied on.

Discussion Questions

1. What is non-compliant risk?

2. What documents are useful for creating a privacy compliance risk profile?

3. What information can a cybercriminal compile from a 10-K Form?

4. What information can a cybercriminal compile from D & B Hoover?

5. What type of vulnerabilities are woven into LANs?

6. What type of vulnerabilities are woven into WANs?

7. How can ISTC practitioners secure transmission of data across the Internet?

8. What technology tool can cybercriminals use to send an organization a malicious image file?

9. How can a printer enable cybercriminals to attack an organization?

10. What known vulnerabilities exist in a Cisco router?

Keywords

Local area network, wide-access network, wireless local area network, global policy, threat modeling, diagram board, mitigating threats, and trust boundaries

CHAPTER 4

AWS Cloud Intrusion Detection and Prevention

Security gateway

Learning objectives:

- Understand what intrusion detection and prevention is.

- Understand the advantages of utilizing intrusion detection and prevention.

- Understand AWS Cloud intrusion detection and prevention.

- Understand the advantages of utilizing AWS Cloud intrusion detection and prevention.

63

© Bradley Fowler 2023
B. Fowler, *Information Assurance and Risk Management Strategies,*
https://doi.org/10.1007/978-1-4842-9742-1_4

In 2012, the National Institute of Standards and Technology introduced recommendations and guidelines to enable the public and private sector to gain trusted knowledge regarding intrusion detection and prevention systems. During that time, many public and private sector entities, organizations, and businesses were eagerly trying to comprehend how to improve the security posture of their information systems and information technology because there were limited resources and information readily available. Since that era, the increase of cyberattacks and cyberincidents has tripled, increasing the value of reliance on intrusion detection and prevention systems as an effective method of deterrence and thwarting the crafty and savvy tech gurus who are deceitfully infiltrating vulnerable information systems and information technology. The National Institute of Standards and Technology continued to update the previously published document listed under SP 800-94 titled "Guide to Intrusion Detection and Prevention Systems (IDPS)" until this document was retired on July 15, 2022. [1] However, you can continue utilizing the recommendations and guidelines introduced in the previously published document. Doing so will enable your organization to understand key functions of IDPS, including signature-based detection, anomaly-based detection, and stateful protocol analysis. Plus you can learn about some of the useful IDPS technologies. While the recommended IDPS technologies shared in this document may be outdated, you may gain additional resources that can help support your organization's need for a reliable and trusted IDPS. In fact, this is one reason why this chapter is important. First, this chapter explains intrusion detection and prevention systems. Next, you will gain some understanding of the advantages of using IDPS software. Furthermore, this chapter shows why using IDPS is important to the development of your organization's information assurance strategy. Additionally, this chapter explains AWS intrusion detection and prevention systems and shows why the AWS Cloud intrusion detection and prevention system is a best choice in protecting information assets. Lastly, this chapter outlines the advantages of utilizing AWS cloud intrusion detection and prevention services instead of relying on another service provider.

What is intrusion detection? **Intrusion detection** is software security that monitors networks, information systems, and information technology tools that send alerts to the designated administrator when a potential intrusion deployed against a vulnerable system is discovered. Unless effectively configured, intrusion detection alerts can be false due to benign actions, which generate large volumes of false alarms. Intrusion detection is either network-based or host-based. IDPS can also be signature-based; this assesses data traffic to find activity that matches signatures established by the administrator. This includes preconfigured and predetermined attack patterns. Or, IDPS can be anomaly-based, which means behavioral. A **prevention system** supports the intrusion detection application, adding an extra layer of security. Utilizing any type of IDPS enables an organization to increase awareness of potential threats and increase security efforts to protect known vulnerabilities woven into the network, information system, and information technology relied upon. This is one reason why the Federal Information Security Management Act of 2002 was passed. This law provides organizations with information about intrusion detection systems and intrusion prevention systems technology, including designing, implementing, configuring, securing, monitoring, and maintaining intrusion detection and prevention systems. [2] In fact, a **network intrusion detection system** (NIDS) resides on a host and monitors specific activities on that host. Keep in mind that it only monitors network traffic. For example, if a predefined incident occurs, the NIDS notifies the administrator. The NIDS is considered complex in configuration and maintenance. Thus, if the NIDS does not match known and unknown attack strategies against the preconditioned baseline, false positive reports will generate. This can be combated by deploying a **hybrid IDPS**. This data collection sensor is a host-based and network-based. This approach provides an opportunity to focus event notifications for all sensors into a central repository to conduct an effective analysis. [3] Thus, it is important that you effectively configure the intrusion detection system. Doing so enables you to set a standardization to recognize normal traffic on the network and what it looks like compared with potentially malicious activity. [4]

A **signature-based IDPS** is like anti-virus software and is known as knowledge-based IDPS. A signature-based IDPS assesses data traffic in search of security threats that match the preconditioned signature that comprises preconfigured and predetermined attack patterns. [5] Unfortunately, when signatures are not updated as new attack methods occur, the signature-based IDPS will fail to assess current threats, which enables attackers to successfully infiltrate the system. Another weakness of signature-based IDPS is timeframe comparison. When attackers are strategic, they can slip undetected through the IDPS because their strategies may not necessarily match a signature that provides evidence based on a timeline of events. [6] Effective resolution of this issue requires network or ISTC administrators to collect and analyze data consistently over an extended period. Doing so requires substantially increased data storage capability and increased processing capability. [7]

An **anomaly-based IDPS** collects data from normal traffic to create a baseline. Periodically this baseline should be sampled to determine network activity. So, if activity baselines are discovered to be lower than anticipated or at the clipping level, the system notifies the administrator. Variables for the baseline often include memory or CPU usage, network packet types, and packet quantities. [8] IDPS operates as an alarm and provides reports that administrators can review to determine the level of traffic flow across the network. When the traffic flow report indicates increased irregular traffic, alerts are triggered. One of the best IDPS service providers is Amazon Web Services (AWS). Utilizing AWS cloud services to create virtual servers (i.e., EC2 Instances), it is simple to configure the automation of the AWS intrusion detection and prevention services. In fact, one benefit to using this service is that AWS enables scanning and analyzing of suspicious content for potential threats. [9]

AWS provides two security and intrusion detection technologies named Cloud Watch Monitoring and Identity and Access Management. Cloud Watch Monitoring observes and monitors resources and applications hosted by AWS, on premises and with additional clouds. Cloud Watch Monitoring enables end users to visually examine the content of their cloud and collect metrics and logs for all resources hosted in the cloud. Management console dashboards are reliable; there is 24-hour troubleshooting with correlated logs and metrics provided, and administrators can set alert alarms. AWS also offers Identity and Access Management. Key security applications for software usage include detection, network and application protection, data protection, incident response, and compliance monitoring. This software can be relied on to render any needed monitoring management and security an organization's cloud dependency requires.

One of the safest and most secure methods of protecting information assets is by relying on cloud computing. In 2023, AWS became a go-to application for millions of public and private sector entities wanting to continue business operations in a safe and secure virtual environment. AWS cloud computing is an on-demand delivery of information technology resources rendered across the Internet via a pay-as-you-go model. This approach of business service enables organizations, businesses, and corporations to lease cloud services and pay only for the services leased. Compatible with physical data centers and servers, the cloud application delivers an ease of access for technology usage (i.e., computing power, storage, and databases). Cloud services are packaged in three types: Software as a Service (SaaS), Platform as a Service (PaaS), and Infrastructure as a Service (IaaS). SaaS is cloud-based software. [10]This service provides an on-demand access approach. This service is offered as a cost-effective subscription with a month-to-month billing cycle. SaaS is important because it provides businesses, organizations, and end users with energy efficient intensive software that can operate on premises. SaaS administrators are responsible for managing service software tools and any application the organization utilizes as its data center or cloud environment. [11]

PaaS is a consumer-created or acquired application that is created using programming languages such as Bash, JSON, Python, and Java. End users have control over the deployment of applications and sometimes hosting environment configurations. IaaS helps with processing, storage, networks, and additional computing resources; ISTC practitioners can deploy and run arbitrary software, including operating systems and applications. However, ISTC practitioners do not manage or control the cloud infrastructure. Their role is to control operating systems, storage, and additional deployed applications. There are limits to the amount of control they have over selecting network components such as firewalls.

Cloud applications are beneficial to any organization, business, or entity because this application enables accessibility from a browser or mobile application. The reliable subscription model enables ISTC practitioners to scale up or down the range of terabytes they need. Terabytes are units of digital data equal to 1 trillion bytes. When looking at this from a decimal notation (base 10), one terabyte is measured as 1 trillion bytes. Terabytes help measure storage capacity and assess the amount of stored data being hosted in a cloud environment. SaaS promises 100% uptime and works efficiently to optimize secure containers to secure data being hosted. This is important to remember because there are cloud security laws and policies enacted by the federal government and Congress that organizations, enterprises, and businesses must align practice and usage with. One of the current U.S. cloud security laws is the Cloud Act (H.R. 4943), which amends the Stored Communications Act of 1986. Additional laws include Health Insurance Portability and Accountability Act, Payment Card Industry Data Security Standard, and the Gramm-Leach Bliley Act. Thus, it is imperative that ISTC practitioners and their organizational stakeholders have legal counsel who can help them understand the significance of the cloud provider's compliance with these laws. AWS helps users meet all federal laws for cloud services and usage. As a federal contracted service provider, Amazon is required to deploy all cloud services, platforms, and infrastructures, usage, and security with the recommendations and guidelines enveloped in NIST SP 800-53, Revision 3, "Recommended Security Controls for Federal Information Systems and Organizations." [12] This policy was enacted by the Joint Task Force Transformation

Initiative and includes members from NIST, the Department of Defense, the Office of the Director of National Intelligence, and the Committee of National Security Systems. [13] There is also NIST SP-800-37, Revision 2, which explains governance regarding risk management framework for information systems and organizations: a system lifecycle approach for security and privacy.[14] Additionally, NIST SP 800-210 "General Access Control Guidance for Cloud Systems" was introduced to establish AC guidance for cloud service models , which is unique from the deployment model because it depends on increased layers of access control, which relies on the security needs of the business operations the cloud system is utilized for. [15]

Although there are commonly known threats when relying on any web interface for business, including ransomware, DoS (denial-of-service) attacks, malware, and man-in-the-middle attacks. Using the cloud as an information system for information assurance will help decrease the success rate of cyberincidents and cyberattacks. One notorious attack method commonly deployed today is ransomware, which is malicious computer software that gains control over an end user's device and locks the device to demand the end user pay a certain dollar amount to have the software decrypt the locked system. In 2021, ransomware attacks represented 21 percent of all cyberattacks and cost victims an estimated 20 billion U.S. dollars. [16] Today, ransomware is deployed with double and triple extortion attack formations. A **double extortion attack** means the attacker wants payment for unlocking the data that was locked and for preventing another attack. A **triple extortion attack** means the attacker also threatens end users with a DoS attack. [17]

The Cybersecurity Infrastructure Security Agency (CISA) reports that a DoS attack happens when an authorized person is unable to access information systems, devices, or additional network resources because this act of maliciousness gains control over information system software environments. DoS attacks can affect email, websites, online accounts, and additional services that rely on the affected computer or network. [18] The DoS attack floods the end user's website, host, or network with seemingly large bytes of traffic until the host or network crashes. This prevents access by legitimate users such as e-commerce customers. DoS attacks result in increased costs of often millions, if not trillions, of dollars annually.

Malware is a form of ransomware. It is a malicious application of code that can damage or disrupt normal usage of endpoint devices. For example, once a device is infected with malware, systems experience unauthorized access intrusion, compromised data, and the potential of the device owner being locked out of their device if they fail to pay the ransom. Malware is used to obtain banking information and personal credentials as well as to sell computing resources or to extort payment from end users. Attackers can access a device using a phishing email, exploiting known vulnerabilities by using an infected USB flash drives, or via malicious web sites. Malware comes in different packages, such as rootkits, supply chain attacks, spyware, viruses, Trojans, and most recently, tech support scams. [19]

To help deter these types of threats from being successful, AWS offers CloudWatch Monitoring intrusion detection and prevention software. CloudWatch enables users a unified view of all relied-upon AWS resources, applications, and services that run on AWS and on-premises servers. CloudWatch gives users the support to improve performance and optimize AWS resources. CloudWatch deploys Guard Duty malware protection log retention, which is applied over a 90-day timeline. [20] Log data retention can be modified as the end user needs. However, this software renders false positives. In fact, AWS admits that Guard Duty malware protection scans can identify harmless files housed in an Amazon EC2 Instance or container workload as malicious or harmful. [21] Thus, it is recommended that end users partner with AWS support services to gain clarity on how to configure the application to decrease the number of false alerts and alarms. Doing so can save both time and money.

A man-in-the-middle attack supports cybercriminals by allowing them to listen in on communications of e-commerce website users. Users are often manipulated when using public wireless networks. Doing so enables hackers to gain access to devices and examine browser history. The browser history can include access to the last online banking transaction or enable access to recently reviewed medical records. Visiting a website that is not encrypted and where vital information is provided establishes a resource application component. AWS delivers quality services that help protect account owners' data, accounts, and workloads from victimization of unauthorized access. Encryption is a key component to securing cloud applications. This increases the strategy for information assurance. Key management and sensitive data discovery also enables increased protection of data and workloads. Additional applications of IDS woven into cloud services include Identity and Access Management. This application applies security management of identities and user access to AWS services and resources. It delivers a centrally managed work environment correlating with multiple AWS accounts and applications. Organizations can rely on this application to deploy multi-factor authentication login features and requirements. Additional layers of identity and access management are also delivered via software orchestration and automation. AWS IDS (intrusion detection systems) provide security checks and centralized security alerts. Continued vulnerability management at scale and security of data is increased. Auditing is provided to evaluate configuration of all resources relied upon. AWS IDS also provides compliance, making sure all applications meet the required standards to operate and share software for business usages, in alignment with federal law and policy.

AWS IDS also provides network and application protection, which enforces security policies throughout the lifecycle of the cloud environment. End users can create private subnetting for IP address extensions. This application inspects and filters to omit unauthorized traffic resources and decrease victimization. Account owners can easily configure always-on detection and automate inline threat mitigations to maximize availability and application trajectory. However, dependency on software applications for automation requires end users to implement plans, goals, and strategies to increase compliance with such plans and goals. When end users neglect to plan the requirements for accessibility to cloud environments, including what password authentication methods will be considered and implemented to protect these domains, they create an entrance point for victimization. Stakeholders rely on ISTC practitioners to deploy the responsibilities they are hired to do. When an ISTC practitioner lacks such skills and training to understand how to effectively implement the cloud as a choice of software servicing, they hinder the growth of the organization. Knowing what software tools an organization needs and how to implement the technology and train the end users is what the ISTC practitioner must understand.

AWS Virtual Private Cloud security provides epic security at the host level. When an RDS database cannot configure its own security group per network interface, relying on rules to analyze inbound and outbound traffic to any IP range can be helpful. The network level can be enforced with an AWS Network Firewall. This installs intrusion prevention and web filtering. The AWS Network Firewall enables web filtering requests at any point, including IP address and HTTPS headers. This helps protect against SQL injection or cross-site scripting. This application also protects against DoS attacks. End users can configure their own security rules to manage their IDS. AWS provides network and application protection, including protection against unauthorized access, potential vulnerabilities, performance degradation, and unauthorized theft. This best protects e-commerce businesses from web exploits and prevents data transfer using malicious DNS queries. Furthermore, AWS delivers AWS Shield, which provides increased monitoring for DDoS protection. [22]

In 2022, e-commerce businesses faced enormous cyberfraud. In 2024, it is predicted e-commerce businesses will lose $20 billion to online payment fraud. [23] Thus, relying on the AWS cloud will enable e-commerce business operations to decrease the number of successful cyberfraud incidents. Partnering with AWS for cloud and cloud security will decrease the potential threats known to impact e-commerce businesses. AWS also offers alternative intrusion detection applications. For instance, AWS CloudFront delivers a fast website interface to enable e-commerce shoppers to create profiles, purchase items, and make a secure credit card or debit card payment transaction without fear of being victimized. CloudFront accelerates content delivery and APIs. CloudFront also distributes patches and updates. This software can be scaled automatically to render software, game patches, and IoT over-the-air updates that scale with high transfer rates. [24]

To increase security and maintain the integrity of e-commerce for businesses that adopt a cloud environment, the federal government requires e-commerce product providers to adhere to the Federal Trade Commission OECD Guidelines. These guidelines derive from the OECD Committee on Consumer Policy. These guidelines provide a solid blueprint for governments while aiding the formulation and implementation of e-commerce policies for the private sector. They also cover developing self-regulatory codes of conduct that include protection of consumers from online fraud. These guidelines make recommendations for increased consumer protection against cyberattacks and cyberfraud. When e-commerce businesses align their policies with the federal government, they increase their ability to deter cybercrime from happening.

Furthermore, it is imperative to understand that privacy and data security needs to align with the General Data Protection Regulation for all e-commerce businesses. The General Data Protection Regulation was enacted in May of 2018, and it requires e-commerce businesses to build brand trust with consumers. Protecting e-commerce users' privacy aligns with the CIA triad of confidentiality, integrity, and accountability. When e-commerce businesses use AWS cloud services, they are held accountable to the GDPR because the GDPR is European law.

As conveyed, AWS cloud computing enables e-commerce businesses to thrive globally and decrease worries and fears about potential threats their businesses face. Cyberattacks deployed against e-commerce businesses have grown exponentially. Thus, AWS has introduced software security applications to protect and monitor cloud services that end users can lease for their e-commerce business. The increased reliance on software applications requires e-commerce owners to pay closer attention to the software applications that are available, and this can improve security and decrease threats. Ransomware, DoS attacks, man-in-the-middle attacks, and malware attacks each create increased cost expenditure for e-commerce businesses. Ransomware costs e-commerce businesses millions, even trillions. Thus, the dependency of reliable automation software that can protect information assets in the cloud requires integrating an intrusion detection application that account owners can rely on. The AWS CloudWatch Monitor is a trusted and dependable application that reduces unauthorized intrusion. When this alert system is configured to monitor traffic in-bound and out-bound, end users can be sure their resources are being encrypted.

Identity and Access Management (IAM) provides guardrails to thwart unauthorized access and to manage the identities of administrators to increase security. IAM provides service policies that enforce permission guards for IAM users and their roles. When using one of the three types of AWS cloud services, platforms, or infrastructures, it is essential to understand what resources are included in each package. SaaS requires end users to implement their own security and policies and to configure the software applications as required to enhance the information assurance of application security. With platform and infrastructure, AWS account owners optimizing EC2 Instances must integrate an authentication policy and manage all password authentication processes. AWS provides the continued support the organization needs to establish a brand of trust with e-commerce consumers. It adheres to all federal and state laws. It also aligns with GDPR and specific laws that govern eMarketing in countries like Canada, where it is required by Canadian law to acquire permission from consumers before sending product and service marketing and advertising material to an email account. [25]

Again, when utilizing cloud services for e-commerce, reliance on an IDPS, such as AWS CloudWatch Monitor, can be instrumental in how secure an e-commerce is. CloudWatch Monitor enables logging, authentication, and encryption of resources. Configuring this application in alignment with the recommendations of the service provider helps minimize the potential risks and threats that target e-commerce platforms. Thus, e-commerce businesses must do their work and learn what tools provide the best security control for their e-business. Consumers must be provided with assurance that the e-commerce operates in alignment with security requirements the federal government enforces. Staying aware of the threats associated with e-commerce gives e-commerce business stakeholders leverage over their competition. AWS CloudFront and CloudSearch are two alternatives that e-commerce owners can partner with to add layers of security to their cloud resources.

Case Study

Berkshire Hathaway's reliance on traditional on-premises networks enables human error to create open endpoints for unauthorized intrusion. This vulnerability creates access to sensitive customer information estimated at 100 million U.S. dollars. If this information is compromised and stolen, it could be sold on the Dark Web for twice as much. If a successful cyberincident enables attackers to gain access to this information, Berkshire Hathaway would face tremendous media backlash and could face legal penalties and civil liabilities. Examining how this incident could occur can provide some understanding to why using the AWS cloud intrusion detection and prevention system is the best alternative for securing information assets.

The long-term ISTC practitioner responsible for securing Berkshire Hathaway's information systems and technologies acquired his Bachelor of Science degree in Computer Science a few years ago and has earned a few IT certificates since then. He is responsible for managing and monitoring the Berkshire Hathaway headquarters in Stamford, Connecticut, which is connected to many other Berkshire Hathaway subsidiaries, led by National Indemnity Company and Columbia Insurance Company, which Berkshire Hathaway Reinsurance Group (BHRG) renders excess and quota-share reinsurance to additional property and casualty insurers and reinsurers.[26] The data of all of these entities clients is stored on premises in the physical network. Since the federal government requires Berkshire Hathaway to share all risk factors publicly, this enables cyberattackers to learn about these known vulnerabilities. In fact, in the 2022 Annual Report, it is conveyed that cybersecurity risk factors include computer viruses, malicious code (i.e., SQL injections, unauthorized access to systems and information assets, phishing efforts, DoS attacks, and additional cyberincidents). [27] Furthermore, Berkshire Hathaway reports that any disruption or failure of its technology system could result in service being interrupted, safety failures for their physical locations, security events, regulatory compliance failures, and the inability to protect information and assets from unauthorized users. Thus, any attacker who successfully penetrates this information system could also cause **remediation** costs.

The ISTC practitioner does not have current knowledge of the potential risk associated with the current network applications relied on, nor do they realize how outdated the software is. Neglecting to align scheduled updates as the manufacturer recommends creates an opportunity for unauthorized intrusion. They neglect to implement effective security methods to safeguard access to the network, including increasing authentication access to a multi-authentication application, and they deploy outdated strategies that also support unauthorized access to this vulnerable system. Even worse, the ISTC practitioner neglects to stay current with the federal laws and policies enacted in 2021, 2022, and 2023. This, too, opens the door for Berkshire Hathaway to face legal penalties that result in fines in the trillions and civil liabilities that create reputational damage, costing the enterprise millions in payout to consumers whose personal information has been stolen during an unauthorized breach of the organization's information system.

To combat this issue, the ISTC must upgrade the current network to a more secure network in the cloud. Doing so can limit who has access to the network and enforce policy compliance that requires all end users to use their username and password to gain access to each level of system accessibility. Implementing the cloud helps decrease the number of successful attacks and prevents unauthorized access to sensitive data that has a million-dollar value. Thus, if the ISTC practitioner underestimates the potential strategic plans of savvy tech villains and leaves the enterprise open to victimization, the ISTC practitioner will not only create havoc for Berkshire Hathaway but all subsidiaries Berkshire Hathaway owns and correlates business usage for through information systems that utilizes the Internet and all current computer systems and applications that transmit and store sensitive data.

Thus, the ISTC practitioner must be informed of how to effectively protect the information assets. This requires the ISTC practitioner to stay educated and continue being trained to understand how to configure software as required by the manufacturer. The ISTC practitioners must understand the value of protecting all information assets and ensure that all protection methods align with the confidentiality and integrity of the CIA triad. Otherwise, Berkshire Hathaway will continue being fearful of the threats woven in its current systems. It will also be unprepared to combat any cyberattackers who are aware of the known vulnerabilities encompassed in the life cycle of Berkshire Hathaway business operations. Thus, how can Berkshire Hathaway executive leadership assess if their ISTC practitioners are staying current with the trends in securing their information system, information technology, and cloud environment? How can Berkshire Hathaway ensure all ISTC practitioners continue learning about new services that provide increased security and automation services to increase reliable of information systems, information technology, and cloud?

Summary

When an organization neglects to utilize intrusion detection and prevention systems, it enables an entrance point for successful cyberattacks to penetrate the information system and information technology. Intrusion detection enables administrators to establish a baseline to determine when a threat has attempted to penetrate the system or when a successful attack has occurred. Neglecting to effectively configure network intrusion detection systems can create increased false alarms that eventually enable successful attacks to go unnoticed. This can create a gateway of unauthorized intrusion that impacts the reputation of the enterprise and its ability to protect the network from continued attacks. When a successful attack occurs, the enterprise ISTC practitioner must share this breach information with stakeholders. Stakeholders are not knowledgeable of what steps and strategies need to be deployed to increase security of the information assets. Thus, the ISTC practitioner must train stakeholders and all internal workplace personnel of the role technology plays in business operations and communication. They must help end users understand their role in helping secure the network from unauthorized users. Utilizing multi-factor authentication login access methods is one approach to secure a network. Another layer of security is upgrading from an on-premises system to a cloud. Utilizing a cloud decreases the risks of unauthorized intrusion incidents and increases the layer of security applied to the information assets. The ISTC practitioner is fully responsible for maintaining control over information assurance risk management strategies. When the ISTC practitioner neglects to align practices and procedures with recommendations and guidelines rendered and enacted by the United States federal government, including the White House, U.S. Department of Defense, National Security Agency, Congress, and the National Institute of Standards and Technology, the ISTC practitioner creates havoc for the enterprise they are responsible for managing. Using an IDPS is highly recommended. Not all IDPS applications are reliable, so it is the responsibility of the purchaser to invest in learning how to effectively configure the software to the needs of the enterprise. Using AWS cloud is recommended because it delivers CloudWatch Monitoring and Identity Access Management. These tools together will help ISTC practitioners enforce policy compliance and improve security breach resilience.

Discussion Questions

1. In 2012, what recommendations and guidelines special publications did the National Institute of Standards and Technology introduce regarding intrusion detection and prevention systems?

2. What year did NIST SP 800-94 retire?

3. What is intrusion detection?

4. What is a network intrusion detection system?

5. What is a hybrid intrusion detection system?

6. What is a signature-based intrusion detection system?

7. What is an anomaly-based intrusion detection system?

8. What two intrusion detection applications does AWS offer for the cloud?

9. What is GDPR and when was it enacted?

10. What is NIST SP 800-53 Revision 3?

11. What is NIST SP 800-210?

12. What does AWS Shield provide?

Keywords

Intrusion detection, prevention system, network intrusion detection systems, hybrid-IDPS, Signature-based IDPS, anomaly-based IDPS, Double extortion attack, Triple extortion attack, and remediation

CHAPTER 5

Enterprise Architecture IT Strategies

IT strategies for enterprise architecture

Learning objectives:

- Understand effective team management.

- Understand disruptive technology.

- Understand change management.

- Understand IT value creation.

B. Fowler, *Information Assurance and Risk Management Strategies*,
https://doi.org/10.1007/978-1-4842-9742-1_5

- Understand the difference between information systems and information technology.

- Understand the significance of vendor management.

Understanding effective **team management** improves how an organization reacts to the implementation of disruptive technologies. When there is an effective team management ecosystem, workplace personnel improve how they approach and engage with disruptive technology. After all, personnel are instrumental in helping the organization achieve its goals, maintain objectives, meet mission desires, and increase revenue. Implementing change management empowers the organization tremendously! The benefits outweigh the risks. Any organization that lacks effective team management faces an uphill battle with effective communication and information sharing among personnel. This lack of communication enables cybercriminals to infiltrate the organization and exploit the vulnerabilities within the weak information system. When an organization understands IT's value, that organization invests in training and developing personnel's ability to value technology. This decreases the need to increase information systems, technology, and cloud security budget costs. Understanding the difference between information systems and information technology also leads to executive level decisions to increase investment in securing both information systems and information technology. However, when an organization lacks understanding of a vendor's business ethics, this too can become an entrance point for system vulnerabilities to be exploited. Thus, organizations need to know the significance of vendor management. This chapter provides research and recommendations for Berkshire Hathaway to improve how it build trust with vendors as well as how to discuss the value of information technology strategies for usage and security purposes with personnel. This chapter will provide information to help you distinguish between information systems and information technology and help you improve change management in your organization. Most importantly, this chapter will help you understand why using the Internet of Things (IoT) for automation of technology applications can reduce cost, satisfy executive level managers, and increase trust in disruptive technology.

Team Management

Team management is a vital component to implement when developing enterprise architecture IT strategies. Lawrence Miller says that team management requires discipline that includes all employees in an organization, which increases high performance culture. Miller believes that team management is a system of managing performance using total involvement of each employee working towards project completion. [1] **Team management** helps describe the organization's goals and is responsible for each employee within the organization. Team management makes everyone in an organization a manager of their individual job role and how they demonstrate their work performance. Team management is most effective when the organization's goals are achieved and there is a consistent low level of human error in the workplace. Effective team management requires good communication, good writing skills, and strategic planning and enforcement of policies that align with the organization's goals, mission, values, ethics, and needs.

Ineffective team management occurs when there is a lack of understanding regarding the roles and responsibilities employees play and have within their organization. This lack of communication impacts the ability to effectively manage a team and protect the organization from victimization. Team management is defined by compiling a list of ideas and deciding on the best strategies to implement to achieve their goals. Thus, it is important to give each employee a list of steps and clear instructions to help them achieve their personal goals, ones that should coexist with the goals of the organization. An example of ineffective team management is when a data breach happens, and the information systems and information technology team is not working in concert and communicating effectively with all employees so they can understand when the cyberattack occurred in order to know how to assess the backup system and deploy it effectively to resolve and mitigate the issue. Research conveys that a successful cyberattack can go unnoticed for up to 70 days. In a 2018 Cost of a Data Breach Study, the cost correlating with a breach was 25 percent lower for organizations that effectively managed their information systems and information technology and the timeline of exposure was decreased to 30 days. That creates a huge difference of more than $1 million when organizations consider their overall average cost of a security breach, which the average time between detection and containment is 60 days. [2] Thus, using these six skills effectively will impact the improvements of your organization's team management strategy. First, it is important that team managers use clear nontechnical communication with employees at every level of the organization's hierarchy.

Practice sincere **emotional intelligence**. Team managers must know how to delegate responsibility and create a workplace where employees can feel respected. Making sure each team player is heard and their ideas are considered, decreases favoritism and inequality. Team managers must understand how to resolve problems and implement firm resolutions. Most importantly, team managers need to have excellent decision-making skills.

The advantages of team management include effective usage of information sharing and delivery of resources. Improving the learning skills and performance skills of employees is important. Most important is overcoming bias. Bias in the workplace harms the ability for the team manager to effectively manage their team. Bias in the workplace infringes on the ethics of an organization, which impacts the organization's culture. The disadvantages of ineffective team management include creating a climate of group pressure and competitiveness, stifling individuality, and wasting organization's funding on team building training that is ineffective.

Effective hierarchy of team management is the following:

- Upper management is involved in both long- and short-term organizational goals. Upper management includes CEO, CTO, CFO, CIO, COO, and the VP.

- Middle management should be responsible for understanding the goals and plans of the organization and possess the ability to communicate these plans to employees and lower-level management.

- Lower-level management should be effective in implementing the plans and overseeing each employee's role and assessing each employee's work performance to assure their performance is executed correctly and they are being held accountable when their performance falls below the established baseline.

Thus, team management is an effective method for bridging the gap of communication between upper-, middle-, and lower-level management. To be effective in team management requires the ability to listen to the ideas of each employee and write down any positive feedback that can help the organization achieve its goals and objectives. When there is a lack of communication, employees often become misguided and lose focus of their roles and responsibilities. Some essential steps to positive team management include emotional intelligence, organization, the ability to delegate responsibilities, and the ability to solve problems effectively. This advantage helps organizations achieve long- and short-term goals. The disadvantage of ineffective team management can result in monetary loss and/or damage to the organization's reputation. Therefore, effective team management should be strategically developed, implemented, and managed throughout the lifecycle of the organization.

Disruptive Technology

When an organization is forced to embrace **disruptive technology**, it can create a sense of distrust and fear, not only in management but employees at every level. Work performances are impacted, and information systems and information technology vulnerability exposures increase. Thus, it is important for all ISTC practitioners to understand what disruptive technology is and how to explain the value of this IT strategy to executives in the organization. Disruptive technology impacts various sets of attributes Berkshire Hathaway already relies on, and any organization currently relies on. Unless the ISTC practitioner overseeing the information system and information technology that controls and secures their organization's information assets understands the usage of disruptive technologies and its benefits, the organization remains vulnerable and incapable of competing with competitors that trust in disruptive technologies.

One key emerging disruptive technology Berkshire Hathaway should consider implementing to increase information assurance is the **Internet of Things** (IoT). The IoT provides service monitoring, production monitoring, and product insight. The IoT, as Oracle conveys, is an extended version of the Internet and additional network connections correlating with sensors and devices that provide effective information gathering, analyzing of the data, and usage of automation and remote monitoring, which provides predictive maintenance. The IoT leverages capabilities, including real-time analytics, machine learning, digital twins, and digital threads. [3]

When the IoT is effectively integrated within an organization's information system and information technology, it helps make top-down managers happier. It reduces the lack of productivity and enhances the tracing of data analysis. The IoT delivers a clear approach to data mining and makes using machine learning and artificial intelligence efficient. There are two methods team managers should consider when determining how to implement discussion of the IoT in the workplace. The first method is using third-party information resources to help cultivate a better learning experience.

Oracle provides a PDF report that shares information about emerging technology organizations should consider using to impact their growth and short- and long-term success. Strategies to increase usage of IoT in the workplace should include creating awareness training. This can be achieved using a PowerPoint presentation or using a Word document. Make sure all detailed information delivers key issues employees need to be aware of and explains how to resolve potential issues that may arise during usage of the new IoT. It is recommended that ISTC practitioners train top-down management, using a digital assessment to ensure these employees are knowledgeable about the IoT and understand why IoT has been introduced and the role IoT is playing in helping the organization achieve its goals. Additionally, it is recommended that ISTC practitioners schedule meetings face-to-face with top-down management to present facts supporting the advantages and disadvantages of incorporating disruptive changes in disruptive technology. Making sure everyone is knowledgeable and aware of the role this disruptive technology plays can help ease the transition for everyone involved.

After all, integrating the IoT in an organization enables it to transform into a dynamic system of innovation that out-measures competitors. The IoT enables ISTC practitioners to monitor their organization's platforms, automate firmware updates, and better manage consumption billing. IoT usage also will transform the organization towards improving how to leverage its product usage data and identify innovative products as well as increase existing usage of current products. Finally, IoT enables an organization to improve how it assesses all connected devices within the office and improve how the organization predicts security issues and minimizes security concerns. [4]

This is why change management is vital. ISTC practitioners need to share the vision of change with top-down managers. This will help the organization improve alignment with changes implemented throughout the organization, not only to technology and systems but with employees. **Change management** helps establish regulations and policies. Change management introduces the need to assess all employees and make sure each employee is aware of the goals and mission of the organization and knows how to manage the information system and information technology the organization utilizes to manage its information assets. When ISTC practitioners implement effective change management, they help the organization compete with competitors and improve its information system and information technology security management. With the integration of the IoT in the office, organizations can improve productivity, acquire efficient access to monitoring tools to assess the needs of top-down managers and personnel, and increase ideal sharing. Utilizing the IoT helps the organization remain current with emerging technology trends and move beyond competitors (Figure 5-1).

Figure 5-1. *Defeating the competition*

Change Management

When an organization fails to move ahead with the times, if the organization lacks the ability to strive for continued improvement and growth, that organization will stagnate and possibly dissolve. Resistance to change is inevitable. However, the change management process is the make-or-break challenge that determines if an organization effectively implements change successfully or not. Change management can be determined using three change management models. The ADKAR Model is an acronym representing various changes team members' experiences as they begin the process of change. Experience includes awareness, desire, knowledge, ability, and reinforcement. Next is Lewin's change management model; it encompasses three transitioning models that include unfreezing, which means relinquishing the fear of change and adapting to change without issues. Lewin says that people need a lot of motivation to change and they must understand why change is necessary. The last change management model is the Kubler-Ross five stage model. The first stage is denial. The second stage is anger. The third stage is depression. The fourth stage is bargaining. The fifth stage is acceptance. [5] Deploying this strategy is beneficial to enabling organizations to train team members to begin making the necessary changes and implementing training as needed. Strategic and change management complement each other due to their method of development, implementation, and managing approach. **Strategic management** is an endless lifecycle within the organization that includes planning, monitoring, analyzing, and assessing the necessities of the organization to ensure the organization's goals are met. Strategic management enables organizations to assess and gain clarity of their current position, define effective strategies, implement those strategies, and analyze the effectiveness of the implemented management strategies.

Change management is commonly implemented by managers who are trying to integrate a new system or project that requires a shift in daily practices. Change management is a process that can be implemented as needed. Strategic management is an ongoing cycle of planning, monitoring, analysis, and assessments. The ISTC practitioner's role in change management encompasses promoting technology but leaving the organizational and cultural issues in the hands of leadership positions. Now that the ISTC practitioner's role is all in, ISTC practitioners are building out a toolkit of sorts, including embracing agile business practices and launching training initiatives and communication campaigns, while burnishing their own ability to take on new challenges related to leading organizational and cultural change management. Knowing how to implement change management to improve employees' responses to change and changes in their responsibilities gives team managers the ability to remain competitive, while reducing information system and information technology vulnerabilities. With technology change management, there is a process that requires strategies to eliminate confusion and diminish the fear of utilizing new technology. When ISTC practitioners take the initiative to introduce new technology, change management is beneficial because it provides a process, helps with decisions, increase analysis, and supports assessments. This is essential to developing change where change is needed.

Thus, it is important that organizations stay current with technology and understand the value of IT strategies when adapting to change. The use of new software requires the need to train personnel in their role and responsibilities when engaging and using such technology. It is not just about strategizing; it is also about planning, implementing, managing, assessing, and updating endlessly. It is a process of growth and development that is beneficial to the lifecycle of the organization, and it must be consistent!

IT Value Creation

The **IT value creation** chain analysis encompasses physical and information processing that is critical to the organization's proposed infrastructure and activities conducted. The IT value creation chain is mapped out in two formats: primary activities and support activities. Primary activities include inbound logistics, operations, outbound logistics, marketing and sales, and service. The deployment of these activities enables organizational transformation of the input from relied-on resources to be integrated in final products and services, which cultivates IT value creation. [6] Support activities encompass firm infrastructure, HR management, technology development, and procurement. Thus, the organization must deploy activities that distinguish it from competitors. Information systems and information technology are two legacies that enable unique transformation processes. [7]

Relying on IT value creation helps organizations identify opportunities to improve reliance on information technology strategies that enable an organization's team managers to identify, understand, and analyze activities the organizations should perform to enhance and transform utilization of information systems. An example is integrating biometric computer login authentication in the office as a method to decrease consistent modification of usernames and passwords to access the organization's technology tools and devices (Figure 5-2).

Figure 5-2. *Biometric security*

This IT value creates the ability to educate executive-level employees on the value and significance of information technology security methods already being implemented and deployed by competitors. Thus, unless ISTC practitioners take initiative to educate everyone in their organization about these advances and innovations in technology, the organization is destined to fail in their goal of defeating those who seek to destroy the organization using technology as their entrance access point. This is why vendor management is vital.

Vendor Management

Escalating concerns regarding products and services offered by information system and information technology vendor management systems forces ISTC practitioners to improve how they implement effective team management strategies to improve enterprise architect IT strategies. This is one subject a purchasing manager does not understand. Thus, it is the ISTC practitioner's responsibility to educate these organization leaders and others within the organization who are not technology experts. After all, purchasing managers and ISTC practitioners are key operatives in helping all other organizational executive leaders determine what products or services are needed to help the organization achieve long- and short-term goals and objectives. When the services or products relied on from vendors do not provide the fulfillment intended, accountability is shifted back to the ISTC practitioner, who must have knowledge of the services and products they recommended to the organization's purchasing manager and executive leadership. When the ISTC practitioner lacks the knowledge of known vulnerabilities woven in the software applications relied on for business operations and purposes, and cybercriminals gain access to the organization's information system and information technology, who should be held responsible?

The ISTC practitioner must have a firm understanding of the relationship shared between the organization and the vendor. The ISTC practitioner must take initiative to learn about the services needed as well as about the vendor who is offering the services. When there is a lack of understanding regarding the vendor's ethics and business practices, the ISTC practitioner establishes an entrance point for threats to become high risk because cybercriminals can exploit these entrance points. The U.S. Department of Homeland Security provides ISTC practitioners and laypersons access to a database of information on every software application product developed in the United States that shares common vulnerabilities and system exposures. This database has been in operation since 1999 but was first introduced via a white paper authored by David E. Mann and Steven M. Christey titled "Towards a Common Enumeration of Vulnerabilities." [8]

When vendors conduct business unethically, their business practices become partnerships for cybercriminals. Under the United States Federal Acquisition Regulations 52.203-13 Contractor Code of Business Ethics and Conduct, Sec. 2-i: contractors shall exercise due diligence to prevent and detect criminal conduct. [9] Researchers in Ethiopia reports that a lack of software ethics can be disastrous to the public. A lack of software ethics supports the ongoing war against cybercrime and cyberattacks. When software engineers develop software that has faults in coding practice, the end user suffers in many ways (mentally, emotionally, and financially). [10]

Thus, it is the responsibility of the ISTC practitioner to research each vendor and learn all that is publicly known about the vendor. Using the CVE website to investigate all software applications is another step that must be implemented to effectively manage vendor management relationships. Keeping a written record of each vendor and their publicly shared reports regarding civil liabilities that have been discussed or brought forward to authorities is another important step to take. When the ISTC practitioner takes this initiative, they are demonstrating responsibility and taking charge of safeguarding their organization from vendor victimization. Knowing how to enforce vendor ethics must be a priority for any ISTC practitioner responsible for deciding what software provider will be relied on for business usage. After all, the software vendor will have access to any information saved or created on the software in use by the organization. Thus, implementing effective enterprise architecture strategies cannot be ignored.

Enterprise Architecture Artifacts

Table 5-1 represents a business and IT solution overview for Berkshire Hathaway. This overview discusses what the ISTC practitioner needs to consider when preparing the business and IT solution quarterly report. Concerns should include details sharing all key benefits of technology and how the organization's reliance on technology helps keep the business alive and competitive. Each organization's ISTC practitioner will approach this overview design differently because its reliance on technology differs. However, the objective of creating this overview is to help ISTC practitioners improve their efforts in discussing these sensitive subjects with executive leaders in their organization. When the executive leadership lacks knowledge of technology and its purpose within the organization, the ISTC practitioner must be the reliable source to educate such persons. When the ISTC practitioner doesn't take this initiative, they make room for the organization to be victimized and technology becomes the supporting aid in this method of attack. See Tables 5-1 and 5-2.

Table 5-1. Business and IT Solution Overview

Business stakeholders	Overview and goals	Business process changes	IT Stakeholders
Explain the key benefits and costs of all proposed IT solutions for the organization.	Share the full scope and goals of new IT solutions with all executive leaders and managers.	Providing an estimate of change within the organization's business processes enables executive leaders to understand what is being implemented, why it is being implemented, and how they play a role in managing and overseeing any new vendor application of technology woven into the daily business process of communication regarding business goals and reliance on technology.	Provide clarity on the type of IT system required for operations and explain how it should be implemented and utilized. This must be shared and discussed with all other IT personnel.
Provide executive leaders with an explanation regarding how the proposed IT solution will change network business processes.	Sharing details about the proposed technology and its purpose and benefits as well as disadvantages helps everyone on the team understand the goals of the organization and usage of each technology tool.	Be sure to create a table that conveys the following details. For example: Process 1 (7 days in total): Step 1=2 days Step 2=2 days Step 3=3 days Process 2 will be 2 days total: Step 1= 1 day Step 2= 1 day	Be sure to answer all questions that will arise regarding the implementation of new technologies in the workplace.
	Explain all essential requirements.	Explain the architectural overview of what will be occurring and provide answers that executive leaders can understand.	It is essential to convey how this implementation will impact the organization financially and in terms of security.
	Explain the impact if such technology is not implemented.		
	Discuss vendor membership processing, including service agreements and cancellation policies.	Do not neglect to share key risks. This will enable executive leaders to understand what those risks are and how you, the ISTC practitioner, hope to resolve the risks.	
	Discuss partnerships honestly. How long will the partnership exist?		
	How much will it cost for the organization to partner with such a vendor?		

Table 5-2. *Duality of Enterprise Architect Artifacts*

Principles, policies, and ethics to consider

Principles:

- What are the key elements required for Berkshire Hathaway to align its organizational goals and objectives with its values and mission?
- Berkshire Hathaway will remain a trusted and reliable product and service provider the public can partner with. How will this be achieved? Be sure to address this and write it down. Make modifications as needed.
- How will Berkshire Hathaway manage product and service delivery without bias and prejudice?
- How will Berkshire Hathaway maintain business integrity and adhere to all federal policy and laws regarding the usage of consumer information, including storage and security of that information?

Policies and ethics:

Internal:

- Berkshire Hathaway will respect the privacy rights of all its employees and customers in alignment with federal, state, and EU laws and policies.
- Berkshire Hathaway will not tolerate discrimination of any kind towards personnel, such as administrators, moderators, and IT stakeholders, in alignment with federal, state, and EU laws and policies.
- Berkshire Hathaway will align all electronic communication with federal, state, and EU laws and policies.
- Berkshire Hathaway will operate in alignment with the CIA triad of confidentiality, integrity, and availability.

External:

- Berkshire Hathaway will respect the privacy of all business partnerships.
- Berkshire Hathaway will effectively secure all website web pages with Security Socket layers (SSL) and encryption.
- Berkshire Hathaway will effectively investigate all third-party associates to ensure they align their ethics and values with those of Berkshire Hathaway.
- Berkshire Hathaway will not share personal information about members' login credentials with third-party entities or vendors.
- Berkshire Hathaway will not disseminate false information that misleads consumers about the products and services Berkshire Hathaway offers.

(continued)

Table 5-2. *(continued)*

What is analytical reporting?

Analytical reporting typically represents the results of a business-oriented analysis of the technological environment in which an organization operates. Analytical reports intend to describe the potential influence technology trends have on the business of an organization as well as the desirable reaction of the organization on such trends. The analytical report utilized for Berkshire Hathaway in this example is delivered in a SWOT analysis, which focuses on identifying the organization's current strengths, weaknesses, opportunities, and threats from their technology perspective.

STRENGTHS	WEAKNESSES
Well-known product and service provider	Lack of trained ISTC practitioners
24/7/365 operation of services to consumers	Lack of trained information systems and information technology moderators
Aware of current cyber threats.	Neglected to audit the information system and information technology utilized
Ability to train all personnel about cybersecurity	Neglected to train personnel about the technology tools used and how to secure such technology during usage.
Capable of implementing new technology systems as needed	
OPPORTUNITIES	**THREATS**
Developing software in-house	Denial-of-service attack
	Malware
	Data privacy violation
	Ransomware attacks
	Neglected to adhere to recommendations and guidelines rendered by NIST SP 800 policies

All enterprise architects should have several supporting system services and applications that can support the ISTC practitioner in performing a SWOT analysis quarterly, regardless of the purpose or the level of the analysis. If a SWOT matrix is required, it can be created using a boundary with two vertical and two horizontal swim-lanes.

A Technology Reference Model (TRM) represents comprehensive views of the whole organization's technology, as shown in Figure 5-3.

Networks	Databases	Cloud
• Servers • Firewall • HTTPS • Security Socket Layer	• Active Directory • Authorized User Accounts • Security	• End-users accounts • End-user passwords • Security

Figure 5-3. *Technology reference model*

TRM maps all technologies and products used in an organization to the respective technical functions they fulfill or support. Thus, the ISTC practitioner needs to assess guidelines that focus on the network, databases, and cloud services utilized to understand what type of information system and information technology can be useful in helping support the organization's enterprise architecture. Table 5-3 is an example of the type of IT guidelines to be assessed in alignment with the TRM

Table 5-3. *IT guidelines*

Network	Databases	Cloud
CIA triad must be practiced in alignment with NIST SP-800-95. Firewalls are managed in alignment with NIST SP-41-1.	Integrity must be deployed throughout all databases. Effectively using constraints is a requirement.	Limited authorized user access. Update access codes every 30 days.
Encryption	**Security**	**Interface Design**
All data at rest must be encrypted. All data in transmission must be encrypted.	All personnel must adhere to all security policies. End user's passwords must be changed every 30 days.	All webpages must be secured with SSL. Penetration testing must be conducted weekly.

Recommendation: Berkshire Hathaway should utilize cloud for storage of all web interface and customer's profile page storage. Encryption must be deployed throughout any web interface and all data stored or transmitted across the organization's databases, including cloud services, platforms, and infrastructures, must be encrypted in alignment with the organization's security requirements. Data encryption standards utilized for

Berkshire Hathaway must include usage of public keys and private keys. Table 5-4 shares IT principles, including security, data storage, network, infrastructure, technology integration, and applications.

Table 5-4. *IT Principles*

Security	Data Storage	Network
NIST SP- 800-53 must be adhered to and modified to meet the needs of the organization's usage of information technology for business purposes.	All data stored in the information system must be password protected with a unique password using numbers, characters, and symbols, and should be modified every 45-60 days.	Networks must be tested for vulnerabilities daily and written reports must be kept with the name of reporter, time, and date written.
HTTPS must be applied to all web pages on every website used to represent Berkshire Hathaway and its business web interfaces.	Encryption must be integrated on all data at rest; this helps add additional layers of security.	All end users must be authorized to access the network in any format and/or approach.
There must be an increase of security implemented with physical, operational, and personnel to maintain effective security overall.		All personnel must sign an acknowledgement form regarding the imposed network security usage on all Berkshire Hathaway technology tools and systems.
Infrastructure	**Integration**	**Applications**
All systems must remain compliant with requirements established by stakeholders throughout the lifecycle of the organization.	Backups must be deployed daily and reports must be kept and dated. Reports should include the date and timeline of all backup transactions (i.e., hardware and software applications, including the cloud).	The application proxy should be checked regularly to assure TCP/IP can be forwarded across the firewall securely.
No unauthorized access can be granted to any system without CTO permission.	Third-party software applications must be kept up to date in alignment with manufacturer's recommendations.	The firewall software gateway must be updated in alignment with manufacturer's requirements.

While there is always room for development and improvement, these recommendations should be given serious consideration with increased usage of information systems and information technology for business purposes. Implementing these recommendations are essential to the effective management of Berkshire Hathaway's business operations and its employees' usage of the organization's information system and information technology. Berkshire Hathaway must consider these principles and ethics and modify the principles and policies as the organization grows and continues adopting technology.

Enterprise Architecture Vision

Table 5-5 shares a Business Capability Model focusing on people, processes, technology, and governance. This table focuses on the EAV related to EA.

Table 5-5. *Business Capability Model*

People	Process	Technology	Governance
Stakeholders (e.g., investors, board of directors).	Assessing Planning Implementing Evaluating Updating	Networks Databases Cloud Servers LAN/WAN TCP/IP Policy standards	Explain the roles and responsibilities of stakeholders, IT managers and team players, human resources, and personnel.
IT manager and team players. Human Resource personnel. Suppliers. Customers.	All proposed and implemented process steps deployed need to be approved and signed off by a senior business stakeholder. Policy compliance must be adhered to.	The organization must effectively manage its technology with the use of policies that demand compliance. Updates must be kept recorded. Daily backups must be effectively implemented and recorded in daily reports with the name of the report author, including the time and date the report was created.	Develop policies and share such with stakeholders, IT managers, team players, human resources, and personnel.
All stakeholders, IT managers, and IT team players, human resources, and personnel are required to conduct daily business functions and operations in alignment with all policies implemented.			Conduct quarterly assessments on all personnel. Implement awareness training and update such quarterly.

People's visions represent collaborative views of an organization. Process is the next high-level business capability because process helps align the steps taken to achieve the goals of the organization. Technology is the third highest business capability because technology enables the organization to conduct daily business and communicate with stakeholders, personnel, suppliers, and customers. Technology and process encompass policy compliance that must be met. Governance enables defining roles and responsibilities and it enables ISTC practitioners to effectively control how their team members respect and utilize the technology relied on with the organization's usage policy. Governance also helps the organization stay aligned with the goals, mission, and vision. The main underlying components of a business capability include

- **People:** The competencies, skills, and workforce necessary to enable a talent base to execute the capability.

- **Process:** An efficient set of processes and activities designed to produce the desired outcome.

- **Technology:** Software applications, hardware infrastructure, and necessary tools to enable the capability.

- **Governance:** Compilation of clear roles and responsibilities plus decision policies to facilitate integration within and across other capabilities, functions, and business partners.[11]

Despite the current threats and system vulnerabilities woven into the ecosystem of Berkshire Hathaway, with persistence, the ISTC practitioner can effectively thwart and deter attacks targeted towards Berkshire Hathaway and its information systems and information technology. Using cloud services, infrastructure, or a platform is a key method of lower risks associated with the organization's collection and storage of customer's personal data. Having the ISTC practitioner take the initiative to educate executive leaders about the enterprise architect IT strategies will enable this organization to continue competing and safeguarding its information assets. When the ISTC practitioner is knowledgeable, they can improve any weakness within the system and help protect the organization from victimization. Aligning your organization's EA with this example is a dynamic approach to implementing a system of governance that is reliable and impenetrable.

Case Study

When an organization first adopts technology as the primary keeper of consumer information, the ISTC practitioner is supposed to provide details about the benefits of using technology. When the ISTC practitioner neglects to share significant details about how invaluable enterprise architect IT strategies are, this impedes the organization's ability to control risk factors that impact security risks. How can an organization improve its EA IT strategies when the executive leadership lacks understanding of what is needed to improve the most vital asset to its daily business operations and communication? The ISTC practitioner holds the power for the organization to beat its competitors. What happens when the ISTC practitioner is not skilled enough and lacks the ability to communicate these essential facts shared in this chapter with executive leaders? Who is to blame? Even worse, how can any organization grapple with this issue when no one has a clue this is an issue?

Summary

Team management is a vital component to the lifecycle of an organization and its business success infrastructure. Implementing an effective strategy to achieve team management can be a daunting task that requires effective change management. Change management is beneficial because it provides a process, helps with decisions, increases analysis, and supports assessments. When an organization desires to improve its information system and information technology, the organization must deploy strategic management. Strategic management includes planning, monitoring, analyzing, and assessing the necessities of the organization to ensure the organization's goals are met. This includes making IT value creation priority and providing executive leaders information that helps them understand the significance of IT value creation. Effective enterprise architecture requires the use of business and IT solutions, a technology reference model, IT guidelines, IT principles, and an enterprise architect vision. When Berkshire Hathaway implements an effective business capability model, the organization gains leverage in securing its information assets, information system, information technology, and its usage of cloud. However, it is essential that Berkshire Hathaway implement effective training for all employees top-down and encourage all ISTC practitioners to become life-long learners to stay current with technology trends. Chapter 6 delivers a well-outlined infrastructure of policy development and implementation that will support Berkshire Hathaway's needs for assessing, developing, implementing, and managing information systems, information technology, and cloud security policy.

Discussion Questions

1. What is team management?

2. What is change management?

3. Why is enterprise architecture IT value creation significant?

4. Why should ISTC practitioners create a business and IT solution overview?

5. What is vendor management?

6. Why is vendor management important?

7. What is analytical reporting?

8. What does a technology reference model represent?

9. What are three IT principles?

10. What is a SWOT analysis?

11. What is governance?

12. What are the five steps of the process?

Keywords

Team management, change management, IT value creation, vendor management, analytical reporting, governance, and enterprise architecture

CHAPTER 6

IT Strategy Policy

Policy compliance

Learning objectives:

- Understand the value of a strategic IT policy.

- Understand how to align policy with NIST SP 800 recommendations and guidelines.

- Understand how to modify policy effectively.

- Understand how to track and monitor policy compliance.

You have gained valuable information and knowledge regarding information assurance and how to effectively deploy an analysis. Plus, you gained knowledge regarding information systems, information technology, and cloud risk management strategies. You have also gained information and knowledge to help you implement effective privacy compliance strategies and you have learned the significance of migrating your organization's on-premises network to the AWS cloud. You've been introduced to the importance of AWS intrusion and prevention detection systems. Having this knowledge increases your chances of decreasing the number of successful cyberattacks your organization faces. You were also introduced to effective methods

© Bradley Fowler 2023
B. Fowler, *Information Assurance and Risk Management Strategies*,
https://doi.org/10.1007/978-1-4842-9742-1_6

of assessing, developing, implementing, and managing enterprise architecture IT strategies. Having this knowledge enables your organization to compete with competitors and safeguard the organization's assets from exploitation. However, without implementing effective IT strategic policies, it can be a daunting task to implement a new approach to securing your organization's technology assets. Thus, in this chapter, I compiled additional research to increase your professional ability to assess, develop, implement, and manage a secure information system, information technology, and cloud environment, using policy as a primary method of governance. Within this chapter, you will review the IT strategic policy plans I developed using Berkshire Hathaway's current cybersecurity risk factors in mind. First, you will review the recommendations for strategy planning and vision. This focuses briefly on roles and responsibilities, processes and procedures, strategy formation, security convergence planning, change management, implementation, review of the organization's scorecard, review of feedback, and gaining an understanding of tracking and control as well as the policy life cycle. Then, you will review my approach to policy framework, policy management, IT guidelines, IT procedures, IT standards, IT policies, IT policy implementation and issues, and policy compliance with my report card, and explore my approach to policy enforcement.

I'd like to start this chapter off by sharing. Table 6-1 which shows a strategic plan to help increase effective security development, implementation, and management throughout the organization's lifecycle.

Table 6-1. *Strategic Planning*

Strategy Vision	There are three primary components you should consider when assessing an approach to defining an effective strategy vision:

- Understanding the need for responsiveness, (i.e., administrators, department managers, human resources, and accounting and acquisitions).
- Knowing the need for collaboration within the organization (i.e., quality management, coding process management, sales, and marketing management).
- Knowing the need for adaptive skills (i.e., education and training for all personnel).
- Defining a visionary board development and management implementation process that is deployed quarterly.

Roles and responsibilities	

- CTO, CIO, ISO (i.e., identify, develop, and implement security policies, data storage policies, and accountability policies for security controls).
- Executive leaders (i.e., policy approvals and governance of management).
- Compliance Officer (i.e., regulate compliance of all policies, laws, and regulations within the organization).
- Data owner (i.e., oversee accountability and monitor adherence to policies of all personnel).
- Data manager (i.e., help determine how all data is managed and stored).
- Data custodian (i.e., day-to-day maintenance of all data, including data back-ups and recovery plans).
- Data users (i.e., manage security policies and processes and procedures correctly).
- Auditor (i.e., responsible for assessing the design and effectiveness of security policies). [1]

(continued)

Table 6-1. (*continued*)

Process and procedures	• An organization's security policies must be updated at least on an annual basis. Employees must be trained and educated regarding all modifications, and policies must be enforced. [²] • Enforcing the organization to patch and update management and evaluation processes. • Removing all access codes and passwords of former employees from the system within a timely manner, such as five days from exiting the office. • Changing all system passwords every 30 days. • Researching all government policy updates and updates of laws annually to update the organization's policies in alignment. • Implementing procedure templates and modifying them as needed (i.e., format, standards, forms, procedure history, information and assistance, keywords, and associated resources). • Implementing clearly conveyed procedure guidelines regarding the development, implementation, and modification of such, including the purpose, background, scope, guidance sections, roles and responsibilities, effective dates, information and assistance, approvals, and associated resources.

(continued)

Table 6-1. (*continued*)

Strategic planning	• The effective planning process should include personnel meetings and meetings with stakeholders to share effective, clearly conveyed communication regarding what needs to be done and what steps and procedures should be implemented to achieve all organizational goals. • Define the vision, purpose, mission, strategies, execution, measurements of success, information security architecture, technical capabilities, goals, and policies and procedures for implementation and adherence. • Clarify the mission and values of the organization. • Determine the strengths, weaknesses, opportunities, and threats using a SWOT analysis. • Plan the lifecycle organizational vision. • Deploy a stakeholder analysis. • Focus on shaping the organization's ISTC future. • Implement a blue ocean strategy. • Implement an alignment model. • Implement a risk management model. • Assess the organization's situation-target proposal. • Conduct an annual environmental analysis.
Strategy formation	• Understand budget cost. • Be knowledgeable of all technology resource allocation. • Set department access to information asset boundaries. • Establish communication requirements. • Conduct weekly meetings. • Oversee day-to-day performance tasks. • Maintain evaluations in written format and update as needed. • Conduct monthly progress reports. • Assess the organization's tactical and operational planning.

(*continued*)

Table 6-1. (*continued*)

Security convergence plan	• Correlate physical security and Information security under one leader as one business function. [3] • Utilize business functions that allocate funding to each department and autonomy that reports to a common senior executive. • Communicate with all department managers and collaborate regarding effective methods for risk control and management across the entire organization.
Change management	• Adhere to the change model (i.e., policy roles, responsibility, and accountability). • Implement effective updates as needed and assess all personnel held responsible for each department; make sure all personnel are being effectively trained and educated about policy and security concerns. • Follow the change model (i.e., create urgency, form a coalition, create vision for changes, share the vision of change with managers, eliminate obstacles, integrate short-term wins, increase on new changes implemented, and anchor changes in the organization's overall workplace climate). [4] • Transform from informal to formal implementation tasks.
Implementation process	• Personnel needs motivation (i.e., pride, self-interest, and methods of success). • Rely on personnel's basic motivations to reach the overall vision of the organization. • Enforce effective policy implementation and strategy planning. • Maintain open communication with everyone on your team. • Impose awareness training as needed. • Set high expectations for everyone. • Create levels of redundancy. • Recognize and reward personnel annually for compliance and adherence to security policy.

(*continued*)

Table 6-1. (*continued*)

Scorecard	• Always effectively communicate what is to be accomplished by whom and when it should be accomplished.
	• Align all personnel day-to-day activities with the organization's overall focus and goals.
	• Measure and monitor all progress deployed to achieve all organizational goals, missions, values, tactics, and targets.
Feedback	• Determine the focus of the organization's goals and mission and set milestones for sharing feedback regarding successes and failures.
	• Assess how your organization progresses and share feedback that can aid forward progress.
	• Recalibration.
Tracking	• Determine each milestone and assess all progress made.
	• Follow up on any area needed to ensure compliance with all recommendations as met.
	• Report all milestones in written format.
Control	• Assess all the organization's objectives to ensure each objective is achieved.
	• Determine if all resources are available as needed, when needed.

Berkshire Hathaway's Policy Life Cycle

I utilized previous research compiled throughout this book to support my approach in planning, developing, implementing, and managing the IT policy lifecycle for Berkshire Hathaway. Each step in my policy life cycle aligns with the policy needs of Berkshire Hathaway. Each steps is provided below.

Step 1: Setting an Agenda

The agenda-setting for Berkshire Hathaway aligns with COBIT. COBIT delivers more than just a lifecycle. This framework is a dynamic method for managing and governing IT processes. The COBIT framework is considered an enabler that helps any organization achieve its goal of policy planning, development, and implementation. Thus, during this phase of the policy lifecycle, Berkshire Hathaway stakeholders and ISTC practitioners can evaluate what type of policies are needed to effectively support the organization's successful function and operation in alignment with federal laws and policy.

Step 2: Policy Formulation

During this phase, Berkshire Hathaway stakeholders and IT practitioners should begin drafting their policy. This policy draft should align with federal laws and policies that help govern and secure information systems, information technology, and the cloud. As previously pointed out, it is important to review NIST SP -800-53 as a guide throughout the policy formulation process, particularly because Berkshire Hathaway is contracted with the government, and this policy requires standardized security procedures to be met to secure any and all government data. Although NIST SP 800-53 is a guideline commonly utilized for federal information systems. Berkshire Hathaway should modify this guideline to define its unique approach to securing its own information systems, information technology, and cloud. Furthermore, Berkshire Hathaway should rely on NIST-800-171 to increase workplace awareness and training for cybersecurity education. Berkshire Hathaway should also utilize the following federal laws and/or policies to help install a structured policy guideline that delivers a secure method of governing the organization's information systems, information technology, and cloud daily usage and operation:

- Federal Trade Commission Act

- Communications Act (telecommunications regulatory)

- Federal Privacy Act

- Copyright Act

- Electronic Communications Privacy Act (cryptography)

- Unlawful Access to Stored Communication

- Computer Fraud and Abuse Act (threats to computers)

- Computer Security Act

- General Prohibition on Pen Register and Trap-and Trace Device Usage

- Economic Espionage Act (trade secrets)

- Security and Freedom Through Encryption Act (encryption and digital signature)

- No Electronic Theft Act (IP)

- Digital Millennium Copyright Act (copyright protection)

- Identity Theft and Deterrence Act

- Sarbanes Oxley (accountability)

- Federal Information Security Management Act (InfoSec)

- International Traffic in Arms Regulations Act (defense information protection)

- National Cybersecurity Protection Act (infrastructure protection)

- Federal Information Security Modernization Act (federal information security updates)

Step 3: Making Decisions

Decision making requires all stakeholders and ISTC practitioners to collectively share their ideas to determine the best methods to implement towards achieving the mutual goals of the organization to achieve both short and long-term success. Berkshire Hathaway should rely on traditional foundations and frameworks of ethics, including **normative ethics**, which is the study of what makes actions right or wrong, also known as moral theory, which assess how people should act. Also important is **meta-ethics**, which is the study of the meaning of ethical judgements and properties regarding what is right. **Descriptive ethics** is the study of the choices that have been made within the organization by individuals in the past to determine if such actions were right and are still right for the current goals and objectives of the organization. Next is **applied ethics**, which is an approach that applies moral codes to actions and draws from realistic situations, such as defining how ISTC practitioners might use ethics in their daily business practices. Finally, **deontological ethics** focuses on the rightness or wrongness of intentions and motives, as opposed to the rightness or wrongness of consequences. This is also known as duty-based or obligations-based ethics. These ethics define a person's ethical duty. [5]

When Berkshire Hathaway is able to determine its policy needs, the organization can begin to reach its goal of defining a security policy that meets the organization's needs and that can be easily implemented and managed as needed and effectively.

Step 4: Policy Implementation

During this step, Berkshire Hathaway should have reached the mutual decision making process and developed a policy that can be easily implemented with little resistance and noncompliance. Neglecting to implement policies can result in unexpected and undesirable outcomes. This is also the best time to make sure all personnel receive a copy of every new policy implemented and are provided the opportunity to discuss any concerns they may have about any new policy, in correlation with their roles and responsibilities with such policy. This is also a time when education and training awareness should be considered very seriously. All personnel must be required to sign a copy of each new policy so they cannot say they did not know such policy existed when they are being held accountable for violating such policy. With nonrepudiation, the assurance that all personnel received their copy aligns with the U.S. Federal ESIGN Act of 2000.

Step 5: Monitor and Evaluate

In order for any policy to be effective, someone must deploy the policy, assure compliance with the policy, and monitor and evaluate the success of the implementation of the policy. Thus, Berkshire Hathaway stakeholders and ISTC practitioners must be responsible and effective in evaluating the outcome of daily operations in alignment with the newly implemented policy. Otherwise, how can Berkshire Hathaway determine if the policy works and how to update any element of the policy when necessary. In fact, continuous improvement of all policies must be applied to every information system, information technology, and cloud environment to ensure information assurance. Whenever policy plans are not achieved, there must be an evaluation to determine the cause of action and a remedy implemented to resolve such cause of action. This should include gaining executive management's support at all levels, giving all personnel a stake in securing the organization and its assets, enforcing personnel to complete awareness training and education, rewarding and recognizing compliance behavior, and holding personnel accountable for noncompliance.

Next is determining how any policy will be managed. This requires continued evaluation of all personnel who are held accountable to the policy implemented. Policies must be reviewed quarterly and updated as needed. The CIO's signature should be required as a prerequisite for policy updates and modification. When there is an absence of a CIO leader, the next leader or manager in charge in the hierarchy must take action. Doing so enables Berkshire Hathaway to effectively manage its policy and assure alignment with all federal regulation and laws. Whenever Berkshire Hathaway encounters issues from personnel noncompliance and faces violations of its policy, it must take action, especially when the violation is against a state or federal law. Research suggests that managers should not dismiss prosecution without reviewing the severity of the policy violation. [6]

Step 6: Policy Framework

Berkshire Hathaway's policy framework should include the following policies:

- Acceptable Use Policy

- Access Control Policy

- Mobile Device Usage Policy

- Change Management Policy

- Information Security Policy

- Remote Access Policy

- Email and Communication Policy

- Data Management Policy

- Documentation Policy

- Disaster Recovery Policy

I have created policy templates for each policy. You can utilize these templates as necessary for your organization. Modify terms, dates, and technology tools as needed for your organization.

Acceptable Use Policy

This acceptable use policy focuses on Berkshire Hathaway Inc.'s information system. To help secure this system from unauthorized usage, activities on this system should be monitored, recorded, and subject to audit quarterly. Berkshire Hathaway Inc. provides a RIGHT TO PRIVACY to ANY PERSONNEL OR STAKEHOLDER. System personnel may disclose any potential evidence of criminal and nefarious activities discovered on the Berkshire Hathaway Inc. information system or involving Berkshire Hathaway Inc. Anyone utilizing the Berkshire Hathaway Inc. information system, authorized or unauthorized, willfully accepts responsibility for their actions and willfully accepts any penalties rendered for any violation found connected to Berkshire Hathaway Inc. Use of this information system by any user constitutes consent to monitoring, interception, recording, reading, copying, capturing, and disclosing of computer activities.

I _____

(First name, middle initial, and last name)

comprehend that my workplace computer and any technology tool used in the workplace will be connected to the Berkshire Hathaway Inc. information system, including the Berkshire Hathaway Inc. network, email server, WIFI, internet, intranet, and telecommunication services and my usage will be limited to activities aligned to legal and ethical Berkshire Hathaway Inc. business. Furthermore, I understand that to utilize Berkshire Hathaway Inc. information system, I must work with the ISTC practitioner to configure my computer according to the following criteria:

- Antivirus software installations and signature updates

- All security-relevant patches installed and assessed weekly.

- Peer-to-peer file sharing software updated in alignment with manufacturers recommendations.

- Web browsers chosen by Berkshire Hathaway Inc. must be updated and configured to deploy the software developer's recommended settings and security features.

- The VPN security settings must be configured and updated in alignment with the manufacturer's recommendations.

I understand that if a security breach occurs on my computer device, my device will be prohibited from reconnecting to the Berkshire Hathaway Inc. information system until the ISTC practitioner resolves the security issue associated with my device.

I understand it is my responsibility to connect with the ISTC practitioner, to remain knowledgeable of any required modifications needed for my assigned computer device, and I understand that neglecting to do so will result in penalizations such as loss of vacation time or days off. I understand that I have no right to privacy while utilizing computer devices or technology tools relating to the Berkshire Hathaway Inc. information system and agree to only utilize the Berkshire Hathaway Inc. information system for professional purposes relating only to Berkshire Hathaway Inc. workplace daily operations. I also understand that known malicious websites are being blocked from personnel access and that Berkshire Hathaway Inc. reserves the right to maintain records of my usage and to provide these records to law enforcement officials as needed. Berkshire Hathaway Inc. will immediately terminate my privilege to utilize the information system should it become aware that I have violated the information system while engaging in nefarious and malicious inappropriate or illegal activities.

Date_____

Signature_____

# # #

Access Control Policy

This Access Control Policy designates the level of access executive leaders, managers, ISTC practitioners, and personnel possess. In alignment with ISO 27001, Berkshire Hathaway Inc. modifies this policy template to meet the needs of the organization because A.9.1.1. requires an organization to document its Access Control Policy defined by business requirements. The actual requirement conveys a specific need to establish and document as well as review the access control policy periodically. [7]

All Berkshire Hathaway Inc. executive leaders, managers, ISTC practitioners, and personnel accept their designated Access Control Policy level regarding access to Berkshire Hathaway Inc. databases and all data stored on Berkshire Hathaway Inc.'s information systems. This need-to-know access control designates hierarchy security using tier levels to end users according to their role and responsibility within the workplace of Berkshire Hathaway Inc. Access control privileges are increased as necessary and security credentials (i.e., private keys) are provided to each personnel and executive leader to access the designated information system database and/or information storage. Data stored on the Berkshire Hathaway Inc. information system is encrypted and must be accessed with a designated private key authorization code to access all security levels of stored data. Two-factor authentication login is utilized and all selected passwords utilized to secure data stored on Berkshire Hathaway Inc. information system must be updated every 30 days. Violators will be held accountable and may face loss of quarterly bonuses, vacation days, or sick days.

All user accounts must be managed in alignment with Berkshire Hathaway Inc.'s security requirements, and access to user accounts can be revoked if an employee is found in violation of this Access Control Policy. All user accounts will be tracked, audited, and managed in alignment with Berkshire Hathaway Inc. guidelines and supported by formal practice and procedures. This Access Control Policy will be updated as needed to meet the needs of Berkshire Hathaway Inc.

I _____

(First name, middle initial, last name)

agree to conduct my daily role and responsibilities in alignment with the Berkshire Hathaway Inc. Access Control Policy. I am aware that violating this Access Control Policy can result in a loss of access privileges and I may face penalties for violating this Access Control Policy.

Date_____

Signature_____

# # #

Mobile Device Usage Policy

Berkshire Hathaway Inc. Mobile Device Usage Policy is defined in alignment with National Institute of Standards and Technology Series Publication 800-124 Revision 1, Guidelines for Managing the Security of Mobile Devices in the Enterprise. In alignment with these guidelines, Berkshire Hathaway Inc.'s Mobile Device Usage Policy complies with the most utilized CIA triad: confidentiality, integrity, and availability. All Berkshire Hathaway Inc. executive leaders, ISTC practitioners, personnel, and department managers must configure their mobile devices effectively to align with the security configurations of the Berkshire Hathaway Inc. Internet Access Usage Policy and be updated with the support of the ISTC practitioner, bi-weekly, to ensure that all external mobile devices are secured and do not enable an ease of access to unauthorized usage of the Berkshire Hathaway Inc. information system. It is also the responsibility of all Berkshire Hathaway Inc. executive leaders, ISTC practitioners, and personnel to ensure proper installation of effective antivirus and anti-spyware software on their individual mobile devices if such devices will be connecting to the Internet and WIFI services provided by Berkshire Hathaway Inc.

All executive leaders, ISTC practitioners, and personnel agree to the above requirements and clearly comprehend their role and responsibilities in alignment with the Berkshire Hathaway Inc. Mobile Device Usage Policy. All executive leaders, ISTC practitioners, and personnel agree to utilize two-factor authentication on their individual mobile devices to increase layers of security to help reduce the threat of potential vulnerabilities that can impact Berkshire Hathaway Inc.'s secured information systems. All executive leaders, ISTC practitioners, and personnel agree to utilize the following two-factor authentication methods to secure their mobile device:

(1)   Thumb print (i.e., biometrics)

(2)   Security pattern (i.e., connecting dots)

All executive leaders, ISTC practitioners, and personnel agree to the utilization of integrity scanning applications (i.e., software) to increase security awareness and reduce threats and/or vulnerabilities. Thus, a virtual private network (VPN) will be installed on all external mobile devices and updated in alignment with the manufacturer's recommendations. Neglecting to align with this policy can result in a violation of Berkshire Hathaway Inc.'s Mobile Device Usage Policy, and Internet Access Usage Policy. Violations aligning with these policies can result in a loss of vacation days and quarterly bonuses. If a continued violation occurs, penalties can result in loss of employment with Berkshire Hathaway Inc.

I_____

(First name, middle initial, last name)

agree to configure my personal mobile device in alignment with Berkshire Hathaway Inc.'s Mobile Device Usage policy. I also understand that any violation enacted on my behalf is my responsibility and must be reported immediately to a Berkshire Hathaway Inc. ISTC practitioner who must deploy the steps necessary to ensure that my personal mobile device is not connected to Berkshire Hathaway Inc.'s internet, WIFI, or information system. I also agree to write down the cause of action and record all details to my best ability and to share such details with the ISTC practitioner and retain a copy of this written document for my protection and evidence of my incident reporting.

Date_____

Signature_____

#

Change Management Policy

Berkshire Hathaway Inc.'s Change Management Policy stresses the importance that all information communication technology modifications must be approved by executive leaders and the ISTC practitioner. All change management processes must be managed and implemented to minimize any risk that may impact Berkshire Hathaway Inc. and its daily business operations. All modifications or improvements must adhere to Berkshire Hathaway Inc.'s Change Management Process. All modifications and improvements must be logged and tested to ensure that all information systems and information technology applications are effectively working and efficiently in alignment with Berkshire Hathaway Inc.'s approved requirements and federal guidelines and recommendations under NIST SP 800-53 for Security and Privacy Controls for Federal Information Systems and Organizations Configuration Management Plan and Control Enhancements.

The Change Management Policy for Berkshire Hathaway Inc. includes the control environment (i.e., all business and IT systems). Key management activities required include monitoring, informing, and communicating control activities (i.e., reviews and reports), risk assessments, and control environments (i.e., passwords and user access codes). This Change Management Policy is developed and implemented to establish management direction and high-level objectives for change management and control. This Change Management Policy establishes an implementation of change management control and strategies to help mitigate potential associated risks, such as information corruption and/or distortion, computer performance being disrupted and/or degraded, productivity losses being incurred, and any exposure to reputation risk. [8]

Scope

1.1 Personnel

All Berkshire Hathaway Inc. executive leaders, ISTC practitioners, and personnel are required to adhere and comply with this Change Management Policy when operating within the organization's network environment or utilizing information technology resources. No Berkshire Hathaway Inc. salaried personnel, executive leader, or ISTC practitioner is exempt from this policy.

1.2 IT Assets

All Berkshire Hathaway Inc. data networks, local servers, and laptop computers housed at the office where these systems are under the jurisdiction and/or ownership of Berkshire Hathaway Inc., and any personal computers, laptops, mobile devices, and servers authorized to access Berkshire Hathaway Inc. data networks are covered by this policy.

1.3 Document Control

Berkshire Hathaway Inc.'s Change Management Policy and all referenced documents must be controlled. Control shall be utilized to preserve current editions and previous editions of documents. Previous editions of documents are to be retained for three years on file in physical and digital form for legal and preservation purposes.

1.4 Records

Berkshire Hathaway Inc.'s generated records associated with this Change Management Policy must be retained for three years. All records must be stored in physical and digital format. All Berkshire Hathaway Inc. records must be controlled and managed by Berkshire Hathaway Inc. ISTC practitioners and audited annually.

1.5 Privacy

Berkshire Hathaway Inc.'s executive leaders, ISTC practitioners, and personnel agree to restrain from disclosing any data resource information regarding modifications, changes, and newly implemented technology applications and/or systems to external persons.

I_____

(First name, middle initial, last name)

agree to adhere to the Change Management Policy developed and implemented by Berkshire Hathaway Inc., and I understand that my role and responsibility as an employee of Berkshire Hathaway Inc. plays a key role in the risk management control of Berkshire Hathaway Inc.'s Change Management Policy.

I also understand that violation of this Change Management Policy can result in loss of vacation days and loss of quarterly bonuses. Additionally, I understand that I can be terminated from my role and responsibilities at Berkshire Hathaway Inc. if I willingly engage in nefarious activities that impact the security of the Berkshire Hathaway Inc. information systems or information technology.

Date_____

Signature_____

# # #

Information Security Policy

According to NIST SP 800-18, Rev. 1: Guide for Developing Security Plans for Federal Information Systems, this approach reinforces usage of a business process-centered approach for effective policy management. Thus, this Information Security policy outlines a statement of purpose, scope, technology to be addressed, responsibilities, authorized and prohibited usage, system management, policy review and modification as well as limitations of liability.

Statement of Purpose: This Information Security Policy is developed to increase layers of security to protect the information assets and information systems of Berkshire Hathaway Inc.

Scope: All stakeholders, executive managers, ISTC practitioners, and salaried personnel are required to comply with all elements of this Information Security Policy and will be held accountable. Violators will face stringent penalties that may result in a loss of vacation days or sick days.

Technology Addressed: Berkshire Hathaway Inc. deploys this Information Security Policy to secure all networks, internal servers, databases, WIFI, internet, computer devices, software relating to computer devices, and telecommunication systems. External security is deployed to secure all CCTVs located on the North, East, West, and South regions of the physical building and all entrance point key cards, each personnel controls to gain access to any Berkshire Hathaway Inc property.

Responsibilities: Berkshire Hathaway Inc. stakeholders, executive managers, ISTC practitioners, and salaried personnel are each individually responsible for their assigned roles in alignment with the job performance requirements each is assigned. Berkshire Hathaway Inc. is holding you responsible for remembering to follow the security risk control procedures that protect any computer or technology device you are assigned. All Berkshire Hathaway Inc. stakeholders, executive managers, ISTC practitioners, and salaried personnel are responsible for reporting any known malicious activities that can impact the security of Berkshire Hathaway Inc.'s information systems and are required to compose written statements that convey details regarding all issues known, including names of actors involved, dates, and timelines, and provide this information to the ISTC practitioner as well as your department manager.

Authorized Uses: All Berkshire Hathaway Inc. stakeholders, executive managers, ISTC practitioners, and salaried personnel are granted authorized access to required departments and technology necessary to conduct their daily business transactions. All Berkshire Hathaway Inc. stakeholders, executive managers, ISTC practitioners, and salaried personnel granted authorized access must comply with all policies developed and implemented by Berkshire Hathaway Inc. Failure to do so will result in penalties that may lead to loss of vacation days or quarterly bonuses.

Prohibited Uses: All Berkshire Hathaway Inc. stakeholders, executive managers, ISTC practitioners, and salaried personnel are prohibited from engaging in malicious activities that can impact the security of Berkshire Hathaway Inc. All Berkshire Hathaway Inc. stakeholders, executive managers, ISTC practitioners, and salaried personnel are prohibited from engaging in infringement of copyright, licensed, or other intellectual property. No stakeholder, business or IT manager, or salaried personnel should willfully share, disclose, or discuss in writing or digital format any business or privacy matters associated with Berkshire Hathaway Inc. Violators will be required to forfeit days off for sickness or vacation time.

Systems Management: All email transmitted through Berkshire Hathaway Inc.'s information systems is to be professionally developed and include the name of sender and recipient(s), a date the email was sent, and a time stamp of transmission. Emails sent from the Berkshire Hathaway Inc. email server must be encrypted and the primary private key holder must be identified. All incoming email messages must be assessed for potential malware attachments and identified with signatures of senders that include dates and time stamps that can be assessed for potential threats. Violators who ignore this vital security policy will be penalized. All data files stored on Berkshire Hathaway Inc.'s information systems must be secured and placed in a folder and identified by the folder owner with a name and date of file folder creation. Sensitive data files should be enclosed with file protection enabled by Microsoft Word. All information systems are to be secured with two-factor authentication authorization access codes to decrease potential vulnerabilities and threats.

Policy Review and Modification: All Berkshire Hathaway Inc. policies are dated and must be assessed both quarterly and annually to determine if such policies are required to be modified to meet the current trends of security issues and concerns. Policies must be authorized for modification by the ISTC practitioner manager and/or Human Resources manager. No policy is to be removed from our database as a primary source for governance. Violators will be penalized for non- compliance.

Limitations of Liability: If any Berkshire Hathaway Inc. stakeholder, executive manager, ISTC practitioner, or salaried personnel are caught committing illegal activities with organizational equipment or assets, management does not want Berkshire Hathaway Inc. to be held liable. Thus, anyone found in violation of this Information

Security Policy in alignment with the laws of this state or federal laws will not be provided legal representation paid for by Berkshire Hathaway Inc. to defend them. Such people will also not be granted bond funding to help retrieve and release them from law enforcement authorities.

I_____

(First name, middle initial, last name)

understand my role and responsibilities as an essential stakeholder, executive manager, ISTC practitioner, or salaried personnel. Thus, I willfully sign my signature to convey my acknowledgement of this Information Security Policy. I also understand that I will be held accountable to this policy and any violation of this policy can result in loss of vacation days, sick days, or quarterly bonuses.

Date_____

Signature_____

# # #

Remote Access Policy

Berkshire Hathaway Inc.'s Remote Access Policy aligns with the National Cybersecurity Society Organization Policy Template.

Purpose:

This policy defines the rules and requirements for connecting to Berkshire Hathaway Inc.'s network from any host (e.g., cell phones, tablets, laptops). These rules and requirements are implemented to minimize the potential exposure from damage that can result from unauthorized use of Berkshire Hathaway Inc.'s resources. Damages include the loss of sensitive or Berkshire Hathaway Inc. confidential data, intellectual property, damage to reputation, damage to critical internal systems, and fines or other financial liabilities incurred because of such losses.

Policy:

It is the responsibility of Berkshire Hathaway Inc.'s stakeholders, executive managers, ISTC practitioners, salaried personnel, contractors, vendors, and agents with remote access privileges to Berkshire Hathaway Inc.'s network, to ensure their remote access connection is provided the same consideration as the end user's on-site connection. General access to the WIFI and internet for recreational use through Berkshire Hathaway Inc.'s network is strictly limited to authorized users. When accessing Berkshire Hathaway Inc.'s network from a personal computer, authorized users are responsible for preventing access to any Berkshire Hathaway Inc. computer resource or data by non-authorized users. Performance of illegal activities through the Berkshire Hathaway Inc. network by any user (authorized or otherwise) is prohibited. The authorized user bears responsibility for and consequences of misuse of the authorized user's access. Authorized users will not use Berkshire Hathaway Inc. networks to access the Internet or WIFI for outside business interests.

Connection Procedures:

1. Secure remote access will be controlled with encryption through Berkshire Hathaway Inc's VPNs and will be deployed using strong passphrases made of numbers, characters, and symbols.

2. Authorized users shall protect their login and password data.

3. While using Berkshire Hathaway Inc.'s computers to remotely connect to the Berkshire Hathaway Inc. network, authorized users shall ensure the remote host is not connected to any other network at the same time, except for personal networks under their complete control or under the complete control of an authorized user or third party.

4. Use of external resources to conduct Berkshire Hathaway Inc. business must be approved in advance by the appropriate business or ISTC practitioner manager.

5. All hosts connected to Berkshire Hathaway Inc.'s internal networks via remote access technologies must use current anti-virus software. Third-party connections must comply with requirements as stated in the Third-Party Agreement Policy.

6. Personal equipment used to connect to Berkshire Hathaway Inc. networks must meet the requirements of Berkshire Hathaway Inc. equipment for remote access and be approved by an ISTC practitioner manager.

Compliance:

The Berkshire Hathaway Inc. ISTC practitioner team will verify compliance to this policy through various methods, including but not limited to periodic walk-throughs, video monitoring (if applicable), business tool reports, internal and external audits, and/or inspections, and surveillance monitoring software. The results of monitoring analytics will be provided to the appropriate department manager. An employee found to have violated this policy will be subject to disciplinary action. Any exception to the policy must be approved by an executive manager or ISTC practitioner manager.

Applicability:

This policy applies to all Berkshire Hathaway Inc. stakeholders, executive managers, ISTC practitioners, and salaried personnel with a Berkshire Hathaway Inc.-owned or personally owned computer or workstation used to connect to the Berkshire Hathaway Inc. network. This policy applies to remote access connections used to do work on behalf of Berkshire Hathaway Inc., including reading or sending email and viewing internet web resources. This policy covers all technical implementations of remote access used to connect to Berkshire Hathaway Inc. information systems.

I _____

understand my compliance to this Remote Access Policy is required and will result in severe penalties if I willfully violate this policy. I also understand that I am held accountable for knowing this policy and all requirements enveloped in this policy. Thus, I affix my signature and date on this policy acknowledgement form, conveying my understanding and compliance with this policy.

Date_____

Signature_____

# # #

Email Communication and Security Policy

The Berkshire Hathaway Inc. Email and Communication Policy aligns with NIST SP-800-45 Guidelines for Electronic Mail Security.

Scope:

This Electronic Mail Security Policy applies to all Berkshire Hathaway Inc. stakeholders, IT managers, and salaried personnel who are assigned (or are given access to) Berkshire Hathaway Inc.'s corporate email.

Policy Elements:

Berkshire Hathaway Inc. stakeholders, ISTC practitioners, managers, and salaried personnel should utilize their Berkshire Hathaway Inc. email account primarily for work-related purposes. Berkshire Hathaway Inc. does want to provide all stakeholders, ISTC practitioners, managers, and salaried personnel the freedom to utilize their email for personal reasons. Thus, Berkshire Hathaway Inc. stakeholders, ISTC practitioners, and managers have defined what constitutes appropriate and inappropriate usage.

Inappropriate usage of Berkshire Hathaway Inc. email includes:

- Signing up to utilize illegal, unreliable, disreputable, or suspect web sites and services.

- Sending out unauthorized marketing communication content or solicitation emails.

- Registering for any competitor's services without authorization from an ISTC manager.

- Transmitting insulting or discriminatory messages and content to anyone.

- Transmitting spam messages to anyone internally or externally.

Appropriate usage of Berkshire Hathaway Inc. email includes:

- Communicating with current or prospective consumers and/or partners.

- Logging in to purchased software you have legal authorization to access.

- Sharing your email address to individuals that you meet at conferences, career fairs, or other corporate events for business purposes.

- Signing up for electronic newsletters, platforms, and additional online services that will enable you to increase your work performance or professional growth.

Email Security Policy

All Berkshire Hathaway Inc. stakeholders, executive managers, ISTC practitioners and managers, and salaried personnel must utilize strong passwords with at least nine characters (i.e., capital and lower-case letters, symbols, and numbers) without utilizing personal information. All Berkshire Hathaway Inc. stakeholders, executive managers, ISTC practitioners and managers, and salaried personnel must remember their passwords, without leaving them posted on Post-It notes. All passwords must be changed monthly. Berkshire Hathaway Inc. stakeholders, executive managers, ISTC practitioners and managers, and salaried personnel must be vigilant to recognize emails that contain malware or phishing attempts. Thus, Berkshire Hathaway Inc. stakeholders, executive managers, ISTC practitioners and managers, and salaried personnel are instructed to

- Avoid opening attachments and clicking on links in emails when content is not adequately explained.

- Be suspicious of **clickbait titles**.

- Check email and names of unknown senders to ensure the sender is legitimate.

- Look for inconsistencies or red flags such as grammar mistakes, capital letters wrongly embedded, and excessive number of exclamation marks to avoid being victimized.

Email Signature:

Berkshire Hathaway Inc. asks that you create an email signature that exudes professionalism and represents Berkshire Hathaway Inc. well. Here is a template of an acceptable email signature:

[Employee Name]

[Employee Title]/ [Company Name with link]

[Phone number] / [Company Address]

You may also include professional images, company logo, and work-related videos and/or links in email signatures. If you are unsure how to do so, you can ask for help from the ISTC practitioner manager. Please sign below:

I_____

(First name, middle initial, and last name)

understand that I am required to adhere to this policy and neglecting to do so will result in disciplinary action that can result in termination.

Date_____

Signature_____

# # #

Data Management Policy

The Berkshire Hathaway Inc. Data Management Policy aligns with SANS Institute Data Security Policy Template.

Purpose:

This policy conveys the requirements for securely storing and retrieving database usernames and passwords (i.e., database credentials) for use by a program that will access a database running on one of Berkshire Hathaway Inc.'s information systems. Software applications running on Berkshire Hathaway Inc.'s information systems and networks may require access to one of the many internal database servers. To access these databases, a program must authenticate to the database by presenting acceptable credentials. If the credentials are improperly stored, such credentials could be compromised and become an entrance point to compromise the database.

Scope:

This policy focuses on all system implementers and/or software engineers responsible for coding applications that will access a production database server on the Berkshire Hathaway Inc. information system or network. This policy applies to all software programs that will access Berkshire Hathaway Inc.'s multi-user production database.

Policy:

To help maintain the security of Berkshire Hathaway Inc.'s internal databases, access by software programs must be given only after authentication with password credentials. The credentials used for this authentication must not reside on the main executing body of the program's source code in clear text. Database credentials should not be stored in a location that can be accessible via a web server.

Policy Compliance:

The ISTC practitioner manager will verify compliance to this policy through various methods, including but not limited to business tool reports and internal and external audits. A violation of this policy by any employee will result in stiff penalties.

I_____

(First name, middle initial, and last name)

acknowledge that I have been provided clarity on the role and responsibilities I embody as an employee of Berkshire Hathaway Inc. and thus affix my signature to profess my understanding.

Date_____

Signature_____

# # #

Documentation Policy

The Berkshire Hathaway Inc. Documentation Policy aligns with the Berkeley Lab.

Purpose:

This policy control is a standard requirement for managing Berkshire Hathaway Inc.'s authoritative documents and to ensure such documents are accurate, current, appropriately available, and approved by authorized management.

Individuals Affected:

All Berkshire Hathaway Inc. stakeholders, ISTC practitioners and managers, and salaried personnel who develop, review, approve, and maintain authoritative documents on behalf of Berkshire Hathaway Inc. must follow this policy. Users of authoritative documents should at least be familiar with this policy.

Policy Statement:

Berkshire Hathaway Inc. authoritative documents, whether electronic or on paper, that specify policies or establish or document design specifications must be controlled to ensure they are accurate, current, appropriately available, and approved by authorized individuals in a manner reflecting the risks associated with improper management of the information.The following controls are to be used in the management of Berkshire Hathaway Inc. authoritative documents.

1. Documents must be uniquely identified by a document number, revision number, publication date, and title.

2. Documents are subject to modification control, which includes appropriate review and approval to certify new documents, ensure accuracy, and update the document as needed.

3. Documents are subject to version control, which governs distribution and availability of the current approved version of any document and approved disposition of obsolete and superseded documents to avoid inadvertent usage.

Record Keeping Requirements:

Berkshire Hathaway Inc. stakeholders, executive managers, ISTC practitioners and managers, and salaried personnel all are responsible for maintaining a master list of authoritative documents that are subject to control. The listed information includes, but is not limited to, the unique document identifiers, current and past publication dates, revision levels, and/or whether the document is considered invaluable to Berkshire Hathaway Inc.

I_____

(First name, middle initial, last name)

acknowledge that I have received notice of this Documentation Policy and understand my role and responsibility to Berkshire Hathaway Inc. I also understand that I am required to adhere to this policy and neglecting to do so will result in disciplinary action.

Date_____

Signature_____

# # #

Disaster Recovery Policy

The Berkshire Hathaway Inc. Disaster Recovery Policy aligns with NIST SP- 800 34- Contingency Planning.

Purpose:

This policy is developed to convey the immediate approach to deploy in general rules for the creation, implementation, and management of Berkshire Hathaway Inc.'s information system and technology tools in the event of a disaster.

Policy Scope:

- Berkshire Hathaway Inc. must create and implement a Business Continuity and Disaster Recovery Plan (DRP).

- The Disaster Recovery Plan must be tested, and the results should be used as part of the ongoing improvement of the DRP.

- The Disaster Recovery Plan should identify and protect against risks to all of Berkshire Hathaway Inc.'s critical systems and sensitive information in the event of a disaster.

- The Disaster Recovery Plan shall provide for contingency steps to restore information and systems if a disaster occurs.

- Berkshire Hathaway Inc. DRP must ensure that an effective management infrastructure is in place to prepare for, mitigate, and respond to any disruptive event utilizing personnel with the necessary authorization, experience, and competence.

- Berkshire Hathaway Inc. personnel must have the necessary responsibility, authorization, and knowledge to manage an incident and maintain information security are nominated.

- The Berkshire Hathaway Inc. DRP must include at a minimum, the following elements:

  - A system to identify critical systems and essential records

  - Mitigation strategies and instructions to safeguard against a disaster. Safeguards should encompass protective measures such as redundancy, fire suppression, uninterruptible power supplies, and surge protection.

  - Backups.

  - Contingency plans for various types of disruptions to information resource and systems availability.

  - Procedures for reporting incidents, implementing the disaster recovery plan, and escalating the response to a disaster.

  - Multiple backup documents.

  - Training, testing, and improvements as needed.

  - Annual and quarterly review and revision.

(First name, middle initial, last name)

acknowledge that I have received notice of this Disaster Recovery Policy and understand my role and responsibility to Berkshire Hathaway Inc. I also understand I am required to adhere to this policy and neglecting to do so will result in disciplinary action.

Date_____

Signature_____

# # #

Policy Management Tools

Policy management tools are useful in helping govern managing policy development, implementation, and compliance. Policy management can help track which device has the policies effectively applied. This tool can identify devices that do not have policies applied. This tool can also monitor policy violations. This tool can identify existing configurations to compare with the desired policy state. Deviation from a policy can be automatically corrected. Thus, Berkshire Hathaway Inc. can best serve its policy management needs by utilizing the EQS Policy Manager software. This software provides a digital library of all policies utilized by Berkshire Hathaway Inc. and disseminates policy guidelines that are relevant to an employee's role and responsibilities. Furthermore, the EQS Policy Manager software allows personnel and business stakeholders and ISTC practitioner managers to review policies and confirm that they have been informed about such policies and understand their role and responsibilities in compliance with such policies. This software also enables reports to be developed regarding the usage of each policy. This is a great way to identify who has and has not completed Berkshire Hathaway Inc. policy training. This is also a great way to assess when personnel need policy training updates.

IT Guidelines

Truly, the most widely referenced InfoSec Management Model is the Information Technology-Code of Practice for Information Security Management, originally published as British Standard BS7799. In 2000, the Code of Practice was designated as an international standard framework for InfoSec by the International Organization for Standardization (ISO) and the International Electrotechnical Commission (IEC) as

ISO/IEC 17799.[9] Today the ISO/IEC 27000 series of standards forms an increasingly important framework for the management of InfoSec. Relying on these standards and modifying the organization's current information system policy in alignment with NIST SP 800-53 can best serve the needs of Berkshire Hathaway Inc. information technology guidelines. In fact, it is also essential Berkshire Hathaway Inc. align its IT guidelines with the NIST SP-500-307 Cloud Computing Services Metric, National Initiative for Cybersecurity Education in the Workplace, NIST SP 800-37 Risk Management Framework for Information Systems and Organizations, NIST SP 800-39 Managing Information Security Risk, and NIST SP 800-30- Guide for Conducting Risk Assessments. The National Institute of Standards and Technology provides a plethora of special publications for information technology governance, management, and security, which are instrumental in enhancing security and system updates that are useful in thwarting unwanted cyberattacks. Relying on these publications as guidelines in securing and managing the information technology systems will be a supporting asset to the longevity of this corporation's business life cycle.

IT Procedures

By using the supporting Information Technology Infrastructure Library (ITIL), Berkshire Hathaway Inc. gets a step up on its competitors in developing, implementing, and managing its information technology. The ITIL provides a collection of methodologies and practices for managing the development and implementation of IT infrastructures. This library delivers detailed data and resources for many significant IT-related issues. Berkshire Hathaway Inc. thrives when it continues being agile and forward-thinking. Thus, it is also essential for Berkshire Hathaway Inc. to align with the service support and service delivery of the ITIL, which includes IT problem management, configuration management, service level management, IT financial management, capacity management, and IT service continuity. In doing so, Berkshire Hathaway Inc. can avoid incurring liabilities that encompass insecure usage of information technology.

IT Standards

Berkshire Hathaway Inc.'s IT standards should align with ISO/IEC 270001 and all NIST SP-800 series publications on information technology. Berkshire Hathaway Inc. also needs to aligns its use of information technology with IT ethics, including practices of ethical decision making and setting high standards of practice and ethical behavior.

This includes establishing trust and engendering respect from the general public. Thus, Berkshire Hathaway Inc. will align with the Institute of Electrical and Electronics Engineers Society. Doing so will enable Berkshire Hathaway Inc. to remain compliant with the industry and better understand the responsibilities and obligations of its software engineers. Additionally, by enacting these IT standards, the ISTC practitioner can better communicate with third-party service providers.

IT Policies

In order for any policy to be effective, someone must monitor and evaluate the success of the plan implemented to deploy the policy and ensure compliance is met with each policy. Thus, Berkshire Hathaway Inc. ISTC practitioners and managers must be responsible and effectively evaluate the outcome of daily operations in alignment with the newly implemented policy. Otherwise, how can Berkshire Hathaway Inc. determine if the policies work and how can it update any element of the policy when necessary? Policies must be reviewed quarterly and updated as needed. Thus, the ISTC practitioner and manager must sign off on every policy update and modification. Doing so enables Berkshire Hathaway Inc. to effectively manage its policies and ensure all policies align with federal law and policy regarding information technology, information systems, and the cloud. Berkshire Hathaway Inc.'s IT policies include the following list of policies previously mentioned:

- Acceptable Use Policy

- Access Control Policy

- Mobile Device Usage Policy

- Change Management Policy

- Information Security Policy

- Remote Access Policy

- Email and Communication Policy

- Data Management Policy

- Documentation Policy

- Disaster Recovery Policy

IT Policies Implementation and Issues

When an organization implements policy, it's important to consider the organization's business size and technology tool usage. Using the early adopter approach will enable Berkshire Hathaway Inc. to assess the compliance of personnel and make updates to policies as needed. In many corporations, executives can be held personally accountable for failing to implement effective information assurance and risk management control. Furthermore, the level of tolerance can determine the level of aggressiveness required to enforce policy implementation.

Thus, it is essential all personnel be made aware of any new policy implemented. This helps reduce non-compliance and enables effective communication sharing between the ISTC practitioner and managers as well as personnel who may have issues or concerns they need to discuss but may not feel comfortable discussing. Therefore, implementing aggressive awareness training quarterly and making sure personnel is operating in alignment with policy will help Berkshire Hathaway Inc. avoid issues that could result in costly liability or needing to terminate vital personnel.

Policy Compliance with a Report Card

One of the most effective ways to align policy compliance is by utilizing a report card method. This helps assess security settings to set a baseline and establishes a value or score ranging from 1-10 (10 being the best score and 1 the lowest). There is also the number of unauthorized changes (some corporations rely on formal change control processes). Too many frequent changes can create problems that impact the entire system or entire network. Additionally, there is the patch compliance report card. This determines the number of patches that should be relied on versus the number of patches not applied. This also requires using a timeline to help seal off major vulnerabilities that may be critical and require fast response time. This report card approach is in correlation with security settings and patch compliance. Thus, utilizing both report card models provide an enhanced evaluation of security control and risk management. This approach should be interpreted as a two-layer factor in deploying improved security management.

Policy Enforcement

When determining the best method to monitor policy compliance and enforcement, it is recommended to align a timeframe with the overall changes needed within the environment. However, one approach to monitoring policy compliance and enforcement is assessing the needs of each policy and determining if all personnel and managers are conducting their daily activities in alignment with the requirements of the policies in place. Having this knowledge will help instill a regular scheduling of effective procedures, such as implementing awareness training and deploying increased evaluations of those working under the policies and being held accountable to such policies.

Tracking is one of the most effective methods to monitor policy compliance and enforcement. In fact, many organizations and enterprises outsource their tracking systems to achieve the goal of assessing personnel compliance to the policies enacted within the workplace. This is commonly implemented with the use of third-party software systems such as the Nex Tec automated compliance tracking software system. This tracking enables the reduction of time allocated to manage all plans and minimizes the risk of potential errors. This software also enables the usage of program alerts and delivers notifications that help keep the enterprise aware of upcoming deadlines or issues that need tracking. This is a great way to track meticulous records for regulatory processes and makes auditing easier to manage. Tracking policy compliance and enforcement can also reduce the burden and cost associated with the process. Just as essential is the use of analytical reports and charts, which too can be instrumental in tracking policy compliance and enforcement. The company should developing a system that assesses each employee's or manager's clarity on each policy to track comprehension and compliance with workplace policies.

Summary

IT strategy policies are essential for protecting the organization from liability and costly reputational damage. Making sure the organization's policies are in alignment with recommendations and guidelines provided by the National Institute of Standards and Technology Special Publication Series is one sure method of securing the organization's information system, information technology, and cloud environments from unauthorized intrusion and access. This increases the ability of the organization to convey its business ethics with integrity and to maintain the reputation as well. Enforcing policies and compliance regarding acceptable usage, access control, mobile device usage, change management, information security, remote access, email and communication, data management, documentation, and disaster recovery are first-hand methods of information assurance and risk management control. The lack of these essential documents creates leverage for external forces to gain access to sensitive data and exploit the vulnerabilities woven within the current information system, technology, and cloud.

Discussion Questions

1. What are three primary components you should consider when assessing an approach to defining an effective strategy vision?

2. What are the duties of a data custodian?

3. What are the responsibilities of data users?

4. What are two processes or procedures for strategic planning?

5. What is the change model?

6. What is the recommended tracking software?

7. What are the six steps in the Berkshire Hathaway Inc. policy lifecycle?

8. What are five of the ten best IT strategy policies?

9. What NIST special publication does Berkshire Hathaway Inc.'s Disaster Recovery Plan aligned with?

10. Why are policy management plans useful?

11. What year was the Code of Practice designated?

12. What is the Information Technology Infrastructure Library?

Keywords

Clickbait titles, normative ethics, meta-ethics, descriptive ethics, applied ethics, and deontological ethics

Glossary

Chapter 1

Bluebugging: An attack on Bluetooth caused by a lack of end user awareness. This malicious attack enables attackers to gain access to any device with an active Bluetooth application.

Bluejacking: Enables cybercriminals to send unsolicited messages to any Bluetooth-enabled device.

Bluesnarfing: Enables cybercriminals to access a wireless device through a Bluetooth connection and collect sensitive information as well as conduct malicious activity to control an end user's device.

Evil twin attack: A fake WIFI access point that mirrors a legitimate access point to enable eavesdropping, by which cybercriminals can gain access to sensitive information and exploit an end user's information without their knowledge.

Denial-of-service attacks: Designed to shut down a machine or a network to stop access and the free flow of data sharing from that machine or network.

Drive-by attack: Cybercriminals gain access to a mobile device or WIFI connection by driving through an unsecured WIFI zone and connecting to unsecured devices to embed malicious malware.

Parking lot attack: Cybercriminals gain access to computers through a USB drive containing malicious and infected code that has been intentionally placed in a parking lot. Once installed on a device, cybercriminals can gain access to that device and deploy malicious acts.

Social engineering: Gaining access to sensitive information from people using their social media profile, asking random sensitive questions, and combing through online search engines to collect and compile data on targets.

Warchalking: Cybercriminals draw a chalk symbol in a public area that indicates availability of a free WIFI hotspot. Typically deployed in rural and urban communities.

Wardriving: Cybercriminals drive through areas to gain access to free WIFI networks to connect with unsecured devices. This enables access to mobile phones and computers (i.e., laptops and tablets) for malicious and nefarious reasons.

© Bradley Fowler 2023
B. Fowler, *Information Assurance and Risk Management Strategies*,
https://doi.org/10.1007/978-1-4842-9742-1

Website redirect: Cybercriminals force website visitors to a different website than the intended one to deploy nefarious acts to gain sensitive information without authorization.

Chapter 2

Information extortion: Holding information storage files and systems hostage via malware and demanding payment for release of that information.

Technological obsolescence: Replacement of a new product for an old one that may still be useful.

Chapter 3

Bug tracking: Software applications used to conduct internal assessments of malicious software integrated in a technology tool or device.

Diagram board: Mapping out the technology tool within the organization that requires effective security methods, planning, and strategies to manage external and internal threats and vulnerabilities.

Global policy: International policy enacted for all countries to implement and utilize as an authoritative framework regarding community and social regulation.

Local area network (LAN): A computer network accessible within a 150-mile zone or radius in a building or group.

Mitigating threats: Actions implemented to control continued exploitation of vulnerabilities within information systems, information technology, or the cloud.

Wide-access network (WAN): A local area network spanning global access to computers and network telecommunication tools through the Internet and WIFI connectivity.

Wireless local area network (WLAN): A satellite connection to a local area network housed within a building and group to enable transmission of information via the Internet.

Threat modeling: Abstracting details to help provide a broader scope of understanding the larger picture, rather than the code itself.

Trust boundaries: Established boundaries that represent controls of information assets, technology tools, and policies.

Chapter 4

Anomaly-based IDPS: Collects data from normal traffic to create a baseline.

Double extortion attack: Means the attacker wants payment for unlocking the data that was locked and for preventing another attack.

Hybrid IDPS: A data collection sensor that functions as a host base and network base.

Intrusion detection: Software security that monitors networks, information systems, and information technology tools that send alerts to the designated administrator when activity of potential intrusion deployed against a vulnerable system is discovered.

Man-in-the-middle attack: Supports cybercriminals by letting them listen in on communications of e-commerce website users.

Network intrusion detection systems: Resides on a host and monitors specific activities on that host.

Prevention system: Supports the intrusion detection application, adding an extra layer of security.

Signature-based IDPS: Assesses data traffic in search of security threats that match the preconditioned signature that comprises preconfiguration and predetermined attack patterns.

Triple attack extortion: Means the attacker also threatens end users with a denial-of-service (DoS) attack.

Chapter 5

Analytical reporting: Represents the results of a business-oriented analysis of the technological environment in which an organization operates.

Change management: The make-or-break challenge that determines if an organization effectively implements change successfully or not. Change management can be determined using three change management models: the ADKAR model, the Lewin's model, and the Kubler-Ross model.

Disruptive technology: Creates fear in an organization due to the innovation of a new technology tool integrated in daily business operations and communication.

Emotional intelligence: Having the maturity to control one's emotions in any situation and possessing the skills to manage interpersonal communication and relationships.

Internet of Things: Collaborative hardware and software applications integrated with sensors in electronics, appliances, vehicles, and other devices for connecting and sharing data over the Internet.

IT value creation: Encompasses physical and information processing that is critical to the organization's proposed infrastructure and activities conducted.

Strategic management: An endless lifecycle within the organization that includes planning, monitoring, analyzing, and assessing the necessities of the organization to ensure the organization's goals are met.

Team management: Describes the organization's goals and is responsible for each employee within the organization. Team management also makes everyone in an organization a manager of their individual job role and how they demonstrate their work performance.

Chapter 6

Applied ethics: An application of ethics utilized to correlate with real-world problems.

Click-bait titles: Messages that can be enticing and hard to ignore and serve as entrance points for cyberattacks.

COBIT: Created by ISACA and business focused to define processes for the effective management of information technology.

Deontological ethics: Puts an emphasis on relationships between duty and morality of human behavior.

Descriptive ethics: A study of people's beliefs regarding morals.

Meta-ethics: A study of moral thought and language.

Normative ethics: A study of ethical behavior closely related to philosophical ethics.

References

Chapter 1

[1] Berkshire Hathaway, (2022). Security Exchange Commission Form 10-K. [Website] Retrieved from `www.sec.gov/ix?doc=/Archives/edgar/data/1067983/000095017023004451/brka-20221231.htm!item_1a_risk_factors`

[2] Ibid.

[3] D & B Hoover (2022). Berkshire Hathaway, Inc. [Website] Retrieved from `https://dnb.com/business-directory/company-profiles.berkshire_hathaway_inc.8b3787830ea77a0fd8fc6493768c68e2e.html`

[4] Singhal, S. (2002). "Computer World: Top 10 Vulnerabilities in Today's WIFI Networks." [Website] Retrieved from `www.computerworld.com/article/2577244/top-10-vulnerabilities-in-today-s-wi-fi-networks.html`

[5] Osborn, C. (2018). ZdNet.com. "Hackers can steal data from the enterprise using only a fax number." [Website] Retrieved from `www.zdnet.com/article/hackers-can-steal-data-from-the-enterprise-using-only-a-fax-number/`

[6] Berkley.edu. (2022). Network Printer Security Best Practices. [Website] Retrieved from `https://security.berkeley.edu/education-awareness/network-printer-security-best-practices`

[7] Solomon, H. (2022). *IT World Canada*. "Another Warning to Cisco Small Business Router Administrator, A Caution over Web Site Redirects, and More." Retrieved from `www.itworldcanada.com/article/cyber-security-today-august-8-2022-another-`

© Bradley Fowler 2023
B. Fowler, *Information Assurance and Risk Management Strategies*,
https://doi.org/10.1007/978-1-4842-9742-1

warning-to-cisco-small-business-router-administrators-a-caution-over-website-redirects-and-more/496639

[8] Cybersecurity & Infrastructure Security Agency. (2022). "Known Exploited Vulnerabilities Catalog." Retrieved from www.cisa.gov/known-exploited-vulnerabilities-catalog

[9] Ibid.

[10] D & B Hoover (2022). Berkshire Hathaway, Inc. [Website] Retrieved from https://dnb.com/business-directory/company-profiles.berkshire_hathaway_inc.8b3787830ea77a0fd8fc6493768c68e2e.html

[11] Security Exchange Commission. (2021). Berkshire Hathaway, Inc. Retrieved from https://berkshirehathaway.com/2021ar/202110-k.pdf

Chapter 2

[1] NIST SP 800-53. (2022). [PDF] Information Security. Retrieved from https://nvlpubs.nist.gov/nistpubs/SpecialPublications/NIST.SP.800-53r5.pdf

[2] Ibid.

[3] Ibid.

[4] Ibid.

[5] Ibid.

[6] Ibid.

[7] Ibid.

[8] Ibid.

[9] Ibid.

[10] Ibid.

[11] "Common Vulnerabilities and Exposures," (2023). Cox Communication telecommunication systems. [Website] Retrieved from https://cve.mitre.org/cgi-bin/cvekey.cgi?keyword=CO X+communications+telecommunications+

Chapter 3

[1] Security Exchange Commission. (2021). Berkshire Hathaway, Inc. [Website] Retrieved from https://berkshirehathaway. com/2021ar/202110-k.pdf

[2] D & B Hoover (2022). Berkshire Hathaway, Inc. [Website] Retrieved from www.dnb.com/business-directory/company-profiles.berskhire_hathaway_inc.8b3787830e77a0fd8 fc6493768c6e2e.html

[3] Singhal, S. (2002). *Computer World*. "Top 10 Vulnerabilities in Today's WIFI Networks." [Website] Retrieved from www.computerworld.com/article/2577244/top-10-vulnerabilities-in-today-s-wi-fi-networks.html

[4] Kovacs, E. (2020). *Security Week*. "SD-WAN Product Vulnerabilities Allow Hackers to Steer Traffic, Shut Down Networks." [Website] Retrieved from www.securityweek.com/sd-wan-product-vulnerabilities-allow-hackers-steer-traffic-shut-down-networks

[5] Osborn, C. (2018). ZDNet.com. "Hackers can steal data from the enterprise using only a fax number." [Website] Retrieved from www.zdnet.com/article/hackers-can-steal-data-from-the-enterprise-using-only-a-fax-number/

[6] Ibid.

[7] Berkley.edu. (2022). "Network Printer Security Best Practices." Retrieved from https://security.berkeley.edu/education-awareness/network-printer-security-best-practices

[8] Solomon, H. (2022). IT World Canada. "Another Warning to Cisco Small Business Router Administrator, A Caution over Web Site Redirects, and More." [Website] Retrieved from www.itworldcanada.com/article/cyber-security-today-august-8-2022-another-warning-to-cisco-small-business-router-administrators-a-caution-over-website-redirects-and-more/496639

[9] NIST.gov (2020). "Security and Privacy Controls for Information Systems and Organizations." [PDF] Retrieved from https://csrc.nist.gov/publications/detail/sp/800-53/rev-5/final

[10] NIST.gov (2018). "Risk Management Framework for Information Systems and Organizations: A System Lifecycle Approach for Security and Privacy." [PDF] Retrieved from https://csrc.nist.gov/publications/detail/sp/800-37/rev-2/final

[11] Security Exchange Commission. (2021). Berkshire Hathaway, Inc. [PDF] Retrieved from https://berkshirehathaway.com/2021ar/202110-k.pdf

[12] Murphy, B.G. (2015). (ISC) *Systems Security Certified Practitioner Official Study Guide.* John Wiley & Sons, Inc. Indianapolis, Indiana., p. 125

[13] Shostack, A. (2014). *Threat Modeling: Designing for Security.* John Wiley & Sons, Inc. Indianapolis, Indiana., p. 3

[14] Ibid.

[15] Security Exchange Commission. (2021). Berkshire Hathaway, Inc. [Website] Retrieved from https://berkshirehathaway.com/2021ar/202110-k.pdf

Chapter 4

[1] NIST.gov, (2007). "Guide to Intrusion Detection and Prevention Systems." Retrieved from https://csrc.nist.gov/publications/detail/sp/800-94/final

[2] Congress.gov, (2023). "H.R. 3844 Federal Information Security Management Act of 2002." [Website] Retrieved from www.congress.gov/bill/107th-congress/house-bill/3844

[3] Whitman E.M. & Mattord, J.H. (2017). *Management of Information Security (5th Ed)*. Cengage Learning, Boston, MA.

[4] Ibid.

[5] Lutkevich, B. (2021). Intrusion detection system. Retrieved from www.techtarget.com/searchsecurity/definition/intrusion-detection-system

[6] Whitman E.M. & Mattord, J.H. (2017). *Management of Information Security (5th Ed)*. Cengage Learning, Boston, MA.

[7] Ibid.

[8] Ibid.

[9] AWS Marketplace.com, (n.d.). "Intrusion Detection Systems and Intrusion Prevention Systems for EC2 Instances." Retrieved from https://d1.awsstatic.com/Marketplace/scenarios/security/SEC_01_TSB_Final.pdf

[10] AWS.com (2023). "What is SAAS?" [Website] Retrieved from https://aws.amazon.com/what-is/saas/

[11] Ibid.

[12] National Institute of Standards and Technology, (2020). "Security and Privacy Controls for Information Systems and Organization." [PDF] Retrieved from https://csrc.nist.gov/publications/detail/sp/800-53/rev-5/final

[13] Ibid.

[14] NIST.gov, (2018). "Risk Management Framework for Information Systems and Organizations: A system life cycle approach for security and privacy." [Website] Retrieved from https://csrc.nist.gov/publications/detail/sp/800-37/rev-2/final

[15] NIST.gov, (2021). "General Access Control Guidance for Cloud Systems." [Website] Retrieved from https://csrc.nist.gov/publications/detail/sp/800-210/final

[16] IBM.com, (2022). "What is Ransomware?" [Website] Retrieved from www.ibm.com/topics/ransomware

[17] Ibid.

[18] CISA.gov, (2021). "Understanding A Denial-of-Service Attack." [Website] Retrieved from https://www.cisa.gov/news-events/news/understanding-denial-service-attacks

[19] Microsoft.com, (2023). "Malware Defined." [Website] Retrieved from www.microsoft.com/en-us/security/business/security-101/what-is-malware

[20] AWS.com (2023). "Network and Application Protection." [Website] Retrieved from https://aws.amazon.com/products/security/network-application-protection/

[21] Ibid.

[22] Ibid.

[23] Equifax (2022). "Retailers and the Rising Challenges of E-Commerce" [Website] Retrieved from www.equifax.com/newsroom/all-news/-/story/retailers-and-the-rising-challenge-of-e-commerce-fraud-insights-from-the-2022-nrf-conference/

[24] AWS.com, (2023). "Reporting False Positive in Guard Duty Malware Protection." [Website] Retrieved from https://docs.aws.amazon.com/guardduty/latest/ug/malware-protection-false-positives.html

[25] Government of Canada (2019). CASL Canada Anti-SPAM Legislation. [Website] Retrieved from `https://crtc.gc.ca/eng/com500/guide.htm`

[26] Berkshire Hathaway Inc. (2022). 2022 Annual Report. [PDF] Retrieved from `www.berkshirehathaway.com/2022ar/2022ar.pdf`

[27] Ibid.

Chapter 5

[1] Miller, L. (2011). "Team Management: The Core Practice of a High-Performance Organization." [PDF] Retrieved from `www.lmmiller.com/wp-content/uploads/2011/06/Team-Management.pdf`

[2] Zeidler, R. (2019). "Security Intelligence." [Website] Retrieved from `www.securityintelligence.com/when-it-comes-to-incidence-response-failing-to-plan-means-planning-to-fail`

[3] Oracle.com. (2021). "Transformational Technology Industry Use Cases." [PDF] Retrieved from `www.oracle.com/a/ocom/docs/transformational-technology-use-cases.pdf`

[4] Oracle.com. (2021). "Emerging Technologies: Driving Financial and Operational Efficiency." [PDF] Retrieved from `www.oracle.com/a/ocom/docs/esg-research-oracle-emerging-tech-report.pdf?elqTrackId=a794fbb9917e400ab81d11a963e338fd&elqaid=88831&elqat=2`

[5] Pearson, Sonia. (n.d.). "9 Steps to successful change management process." [Website] Retrieved from `https://tallyfy.com/change-management-process/`

[6] Piccoli, G. & Pigni, F. (2019). *Information Systems for Managers (4thEd)*. Prospect Press, Burlington, VT., p. 218

[7] Ibid.

[8] CVE.mitre.org (2023). History. [Website] Retrieved from www.cve.org/About/History

[9] Acquisition.gov (2023). 52.203-13 "Contractor Code of Business Ethics and Conduct." [Website] Retrieved from www.acquisition.gov/far/52.203-13

[10] Biable, E.S., Garcia, M.N., Midekso, D., and Pombo, N. (2022). "Ethical Issues in Software Requirements Engineering." [PDF] Retrieved from www.semanticscholar.org/paper/Ethical-Issues-in-Software-Requirements-Engineering-Biable-Garcia/4c1f60839ce4bb61577d218c2f1f30f8373b24f6

[11] Ambrosio, A. (2020). *Digitalist Magazine.* "The Business Capability Model." [Website] Retrieved from www.digitalistmag.com/digital-economy/2020/02/12/business-capability-model-06202703/

Chapter 6

[1] Johnson, R. (2015). *Security Policies and Implementation Issues. (2nd Ed).* Jones & Bartlett Learning, Burlington, MA., p. 133

[2] Whitman, E.M. & Mattord, J.H. (2017). *Management of Information Security. (5th Ed).* Cengage Learning, Boston, MA., p. 372

[3] Ibid.

[4] Johnson, R. (2015). *Security Policies and Implementation Issues. (2nd Ed).* Jones & Bartlett Learning, Burlington, MA.

[5] Whitman, E.M. & Mattord, J.H. (2017). *Management of Information Security (5th Ed).* Cengage Learning, Boston, MA.

[6] Ibid.

[7] Access Control Policy. (2016). "ISO 27001 Access Control Policy Examples" [Website] Retrieved from http://iso27001guide.com/annex-a/access-control/business-requirements-access-control/iso-27001-access-control-policy-examples/

[8] Preteshbiwas, (2020). ISO Consultant in Kuwait. [Website] Retrieved from https://isoconsultantkuwait.com/2020/02/01/example-of-change-management-policy-and-procedure/

[9] Whitman, E.M. & Mattord, J.H. (2017). *Management of Information Security. (5th Ed)*. Cengage Learning, Boston, MA., p. 372

Index

A

Acceptable use policy, 108, 109
Access Control Policy, 109, 110
ADKAR model, 83
Analytical reporting, 90
Anomaly-based IDPS, 66
Applied ethics, 105
AWS cloud computing, 66, 71
AWS CloudWatch Monitor, 72
AWS intrusion detection systems (IDS), 22, 65, 69, 70, 75
AWS Network Firewall, 70
AWS Virtual Private Cloud security, 70

B

Berkshire Hathaway Inc., 3, 4, 7–9, 13, 14, 18, 29, 35, 36, 41–43, 81, 94, 95
    acceptable use policy, 108
    Access Control Policy, 109, 110
    assessments and auditing, 13
    business practices, 29
    Change Management Policy, 112
    Data Management Policy, 121
    Disaster Recovery Policy, 123, 125
    Documentation Policy, 122, 123
    Electronic Mail Security Policy, 118
    Email and Communication Policy, 118
    Email Security Policy, 119, 120
    Form 10-K Annual Report, 40
    information profile chart, 18
    information security policy, 114, 116
    information system, 73, 108
    ISTC practitioners, 60, 61
    IT policies, 127
    IT policies implementation and issues, 128
    IT procedures, 126
    IT standards, 126
    Mobile Device Usage Policy, 110, 111
    policy compliance with report card, 128
    policy management tools, 125
    privacy issues imbacting, 43, 44
    quarterly assessments of IT practitioners, 13
    Remote Access Policy, 116–118
    risk factors, 9–12
    scope, 112, 113
    security breach, 108
Berkshire Hathaway Reinsurance Group (BHRG), 73
Biometric security, 85
Bluebugging, 8
Bluejacking, 8
Bluesnarfing, 8
Bug tracking systems, 58
Business capability model, 93, 95

C

Change management, 82–84, 95, 102
Change Management Policy, 112, 113
Clickbait titles, 120

145

© Bradley Fowler 2023
B. Fowler, *Information Assurance and Risk Management Strategies*,
https://doi.org/10.1007/978-1-4842-9742-1

GPSR Compliance
The European Union's (EU) General Product Safety Regulation (GPSR) is a set
of rules that requires consumer products to be safe and our obligations to
ensure this.

If you have any concerns about our products, you can contact us on

ProductSafety@springernature.com

In case Publisher is established outside the EU, the EU authorized
representative is:

Springer Nature Customer Service Center GmbH
Europaplatz 3
69115 Heidelberg, Germany